NONE AGAINST!

NONE AGAINST!

Keith Magnuson

with Robert Bradford

ILLUSTRATED WITH PHOTOGRAPHS

DODD, MEAD & COMPANY

NEW YORK

ISBN: 0–396–06702–6
Library of Congress Catalog Card Number: 72–3933

*Printed in the United States of America
by The Cornwall Press, Inc., Cornwall, N. Y.*

To my family, my friends, and the game

Editor's Foreword

Greater Chicago in the spring. Stanley Cup time. Tulips and magnolias blooming. Climate seductively warm for hockey. Final efforts are being made to juggle and do lasting justice to an enormous volume of instructive, outrageously funny yet grimly realistic Magnuson notes.

Here's a pile of scrapbooks tracing back to nursing nipples. Childhood ribbons won in skating potato races. A third-grade report from a piano teacher declaring a heavy left hand to be stronger than the right. A Sunday School sermon card, on the back of which appears in a young and wavy scrawl: "Rules That Good Defencemen Follow . . ." It's quite a list for a ten-year-old.

Editor's Foreword

Here's an old purchase order for an early stamp and coin collection still very much alive today. Here, in fact, is almost everything relating to the remarkable young career of 24-year-old Keith Arlen Magnuson, All-Star Defenseman for the Chicago Black Hawks, hockey's latest and most prolific "hit man."

But Keith is also articulate. And, over the course of our collaboration, my only real surprise was in discovering exactly how spontaneous, how honest and how compelling he actually turned out to be. Maggy emerges from his ultraviolent profession as one of the most sensitive and eager wits I can imagine: a tenfold Thanksgiving spread on a single smorgasbord.

The phone rings. A familiar voice apologizes for being late to dinner. Maggy is apartment hunting. His perennial roommate and fellow Black Hawk, Cliff Koroll, is about to be married. They were college roommates, too, back at Denver University when the hockey team won back-to-back NCAA championships, with Cliff as captain one year, Keith the next. Friends call them "The Odd Couple." They were boyhood friends, as well, even further back in Saskatoon, where they first met head-on playing hockey. Neither has ever been on a losing team in his entire life.

But now "The Odd Couple" is breaking up after all these years. And in the thick of the present nuptial excitement, there's the faintest trace of sadness. Maggy never says so any more than he'll admit to playing with a painful knee injury for half a season or wearing a cast on his wrist inside the glove. It's just a fleeting, wavering moment in his voice. And now, on the phone, it's gone.

Writing can be a pretty lonely task after all the fun of talking. But never in this writer's experience has such loyalty and genuine interest been afforded by the other side when this lonely task began, which tells you something pretty basic about the person and his book.

The personal, off-ice side of Magnuson is something that few people ever get to see. Here are the phone calls back to Saskatchewan after games: "Hi, Dad, is Mom still awake?" together with his professional philosophy: "It's not what you make, it's what you keep."

The last may in some way explain Keith visiting blind children's homes, to tell the children how the game of hockey *feels*. Or his "seminar" in a paraplegic rehabilitation center, teaching the patients how to stick-handle from their wheelchairs while sitting in one himself.

One last thing: During the course of this entire project, no blows were struck. Not even once.

—R. H. BRADFORD

Chicago, Illinois

Contents

1. Confessions of a "Hit Man"   *1*

2. Canadian Gothic   *47*

3. Saskatoon   *71*

4. Murray, Denver and Dawn   *82*

5. Harry and Me   *118*

6. The Riddler   *137*

7. Inside a Team   *152*

I received this from a fan at the beginning of Stanley Cup, 1971:

> "For over a thousand years, Roman conquerors returning from the wars enjoyed the honor of the triumph, the tumultuous parade. In the procession came trumpeters, musicians and strange animals from the conquered territories, together with carts laden with treasure and captured armaments.
>
> "The conqueror rode in a triumphal chariot, the dazed prisoners walking in chains before him. Sometimes his children, robed in white, stood with him in the chariot or rode the trace horses in front. A slave was close beside, holding a golden crown and whispering in the conqueror's ear a warning . . . that all glory is but fleeting."
>
> —*Anonymous*

CHAPTER *1*

Confessions of a "Hit Man"

"Cripes! That Magnuson kid sure gets psyched up," my opponents claim—and, of course, they're dead right. Because for me to take the violent world of professional hockey any differently would be dead wrong. I'm totally serious, totally committed to the game. Besides, I can't play it any other way; I'm a "hit man."

I once read somewhere that in a typically rough National Hockey League month there were broken jaws, concussions, skull fractures, innumerable painful bruises and contusions, as well as about 700 stitches dealt out. I can believe it. Long ago I gave up counting the stitches above my own neck when I reached 250. And when I'm tired, all that scar tissue starts to twitch and burn, little nerve pains flitting across my face and around my head. Sometimes I even joke about getting spastic fits as a much older man. But I'm not complaining.

I recall my first training camp trial with the Chicago Black Hawks in 1969. I'd just graduated from Denver University with a degree in business administration, although I actually majored more in hockey than anything else. Prior to this time, I know of no modern college graduate who had ever gone straight into the pros as a regular. In fact, completing your education while playing college-brand hockey had always been considered by Canadians as the surest way *not* to make the NHL. So here I was, hoping to change all that.

For four years I'd been training and playing in that thin, clear air of the Rocky Mountains, building up my lungs. Consequently, though I was still a naive, gullible, red-haired Western Canadian kid, sure as hell scared at my first pro camp, I nevertheless felt in better shape than anyone there.

Of course, like every young Canadian I considered the NHL staffed with demi-gods. And Chicago had some of the best. But I soon realized that all these guys —even Bobby and Stan, Whitey and Chico—were human, and made mistakes too. At least that's what I kept telling myself all that week, lying on my bed in the same lonely little hotel room each rookie prospect finds himself staying in. Right then I determined that if I didn't make this team on my ability, I'd make it on my desire. No one had come to play more than I.

Early in the week Coach Billy Reay skated over to me during a morning practice session. "It's going to be a long season, kid. You shouldn't work so hard."

"But I always work hard," I told him, which probably sounded cocky but is true. Hard work—and its rewards—has been the story of my life. And if I didn't push myself harder than most people and get fired up on the ice, I would never have made the Black Hawks, been picked as an All-Star these last two years, or probably even be playing at all. For as long as I can remember, aggressive spirit has had to compensate for certain talents I lack—and I lack plenty.

To begin with, I have the ugliest feet on the Black Hawks. Before a game we all pay a visit to the dressing room commode to make ourselves as light as possible. You can't see who's next to you through the partition, but everyone can always recognize Magnuson by his big, ugly feet. My left foot is bigger than my right, and though I wear standard size 11 shoes, I have specially made skates half a size apart. Like many players, especially my teammate Bill White whose toes are all crumpled up, I want my skates to be very tight.

I'm the only Black Hawk who doesn't wear socks. I like the extra touch of leather on bare skin for the same reason a car racer wears tight driving gloves. I like to feel every part of the ice. The trouble is that our equipment manager, Louie Varga, is always painting our skates with a black, waterproofing glop that gets all over my feet. So I carry a little toebrush for cleaning my nails—that Swedish instinct for cleanliness. Louie likes to kid me about this, which is funny when you get to know what a disorganized and scatterbrained person I really am. He's always remembering that toebrush when I've forgotten to pack it.

Even when my feet are clean, they're almost blue from prominent veins that stand out all over my lower legs and ankles, something I like to think comes from hard work. But my brother, a doctor, says I inherited these from my dad, who grew up wearing tight shoes because his parents could seldom afford new ones. Some are varicose veins and run together in little blue knots. Nothing serious, but something I think I'll have operated on someday. One thing for sure—I don't flash my feet around pools, and I never wear Bermuda shorts.

That's another thing. My legs. I've always been self-conscious about them. They're small, and so are my calves. For 24 years I've worked on them, but they're just not getting any bigger. Sometimes I stand and look in the mirror of the suburban Chicago apartment I share with my teammate and former college roommate, Cliff Koroll. Truthfully, my physique is rather bad; only the big skating muscles in my thighs give any proportion at all to my body.

Bobby Hull once said that Chico Maki and I could never get by each other if we met in a hallway—we're both so bow-legged. And our trainer, Skip Thayer,

4

who's not exactly an Adonis himself, says that if I ever straighten out my legs, I'll be the tallest defenseman in the league.

True. I walk with a slouch. All the Magnusons do. I remember in grade school back in Saskatchewan, just after we'd moved from tiny Wadena to Saskatoon, some neighbors who'd known my family saw me walking to school one day. They'd never met me, but they said they knew I was a Magnuson by my slouch. It's the same way I skate—like my older brothers Wayne the musician and Dale the doctor, who were both great natural athletes at school. I never was, and I always regarded my brothers as supermen. So did the rest of the province. It always got around when the "Magnuson boys" were in town. At college my teammates used to kid me about needing knuckle pads to keep my large fists from scraping on the ground. And Cliff still says I look like a Cro-Magnon man.

I work like hell on my deficiencies all the time. Every night I go through a vigorous exercise routine with special emphasis on my legs. Five minutes of loosening and stretching: bending, arm circles, that kind of thing. Then I do calf-raises, lifting my 190 pounds up on my toes, trying to increase the number each day, but doing only one round of everything so I won't be too tired for practice the next morning. Then I run in place for a bit with 5- to 10-pound weights strapped to my ankles.

I'm a weight freak. I use extra weights for everything—weighted pucks and weights on my skates in practice; barbell sets, exercycles and all sorts of devices in my room. I depend on them.

Running in place keeps my stomach tight. I also concentrate on wrist work, which is very important for hockey players. I have this pulley rig with a weight on the end of a rope, which I twist up and let down with my arms straight out in front of me. Then I reverse the direction. I do this as many times as I can before moving to the springs—the kind you pull apart—good for the *latissimus dorsi* muscles along the ribs, called "lats." It also strengthens my shoulder, which I dislocated playing lacrosse back in college.

For the chest and triceps I do 15 seconds of isometric curls. I grab some immovable object and pull up with a steady pressure, letting my energy flow from the bottoms of my arms. Then come push-ups and sit-ups, essential for building overall strength. My chest is about 44 inches and my waist a reasonably trim 33. But like most hockey players, I have a big ass, which comes from skating all the time. That's where all our power originates, from the *gluteus maximus*, the "gluts." And these must be kept as tight as possible.

Lastly, I box for a while—just shadow boxing the same as I do on the ice after practice. I get so lost in my private routine sometimes that Skip Thayer has to kick me off the rink when he discovers me shadow boxing my reflection in a glass dasher panel long after practice ends.

Confessions of a "Hit Man"

I just throw punches, keeping my chin in. Then counter-punch, making sure my jab comes straight back and doesn't fall down. When you box you turn sideways to make yourself less of a target. You also keep that leading wrist taut so it will snap at just the right moment—*snap! snap! snap!* with a few fast jabs. Then you bring the jab hand back and hit with your power—*boom*—from the other side. Then back to the jab again. But you've got to have rhythm, perfect timing, to start your opponent moving back and to keep him there while you close in on him.

Toronto's Connie Smythe once said, "If you can beat them in the alley, you can beat them on the ice." But that was before the new third-man rule put a damper on gang-style hockey brawls, the kind Boston used to like so much. Yet I'm certain that in a real one-on-one hockey fight, something you seldom see, good form will win out. Anyway, I'll be ready for the test.

Well, Skip may stand there a few moments watching all this, then he says, "Building up your confidence again, eh Maggie? Fighting someone where you know you can't lose." Thanks, Skip.

When we were first roommates, Cliff used to wonder late at night what the hell was going on. Here I'd be clanking around the apartment with weights all over me. And one night when I had a date staying late but was still going through my routine, he simply couldn't believe it.

We kid each other a lot. I talk about his big ears and

he calls me "Lips." But he never laughs at my legs. Maybe it's because of those huge Slavic field worker calves of his. Actually, however, Cliff knows exactly why I'm so serious about all this body stuff. And it's for this reason that he never really rubs it in.

The fact is, the only time I was ever *naturally* good at anything was in the first grade when I was big for my age and the fastest runner in my class. Then in the second, third and fourth grades, I kept becoming slower . . . and smaller. I worried like hell, until one day it occurred to me that everyone else was growing up and getting faster, while I was still staying just the same.

But Dad always said that if you work for something hard enough, with God's help you'll attain it. And often I've found this to be absolutely right (though I've fallen far from the austere standards of the strict Canadian Baptist faith I was raised in).

When I began throwing the javelin in junior high school, for example, I couldn't get it beyond 90 feet. The coach just about gave up. But not me. At night I'd go down to the cellar and work on my pulley-weight-arm strengthener for hours. Eventually, in high school, I won the javelin championship of the province.

The same with football. I was always small for the team. In my freshman year in high school the coach kept me on the squad as a third-string quarterback purely out of sympathy. I never played a minute. But every Sunday, after watching the NFL on television

8

(TV was just arriving out there), I'd go outside by myself to play quarterback—throwing at a screen, doing the jump-pass bit, fading back and releasing. The next year I opened at quarterback, and we won the city championship.

Baseball and lacrosse were no different. Nothing came easy until I'd worked my buns off. Either I lacked the strength or the natural ability. Something was always wrong. Even in hockey I had to work like the devil on my skating because I was slow and my shot wasn't any good—in fact, it still isn't.

Cliff and I were recently in a TV bit on our bachelor pad. The camera panned his room, closing in on the zebra painting above his bed and the matching bedspread and all the important goal pucks he's scored in the NHL, including his first hat-trick. (They hadn't yet reached my bedroom with its imitation leopard motif.)

"Oh my! What a lot of pucks up there, eh Cliff?" I was trying to be smart.

"Yeah," he shot back with his prairie-wide grin. "More than you'll ever know, Maggy."

I'd only scored three goals in my entire NHL career up to that time, and I've only scored three since. He still kids me about having the weakest shot in Saskatchewan—that's where we first met, on a rink in Saskatoon, playing on opposite teams. Even then he was about the same size ox he is today. He remembers me as that little runt who kept running into him and falling down. But I always got back up again.

The truth is that I recognize my weaknesses and am my own worst critic. That I'm a perfectionist really tops things off. During games when I'm on the bench typically standing up, yelling, leaning out over the boards, teammates will say, "Take it easy, Mag. Don't get so excited." Maybe they're right, but I've tried staying calm and just can't do it. It's not my natural state. On the ice I'm basically a worry wart. And though it's important to have some notion of your own limitations, I really believe the past is nothing; that everything lies in the future. You're as good as your next shift, I like to think. That's why I'm nowhere near my playing potential and have never stopped to ponder the extent of my own limitations. I can't afford to. I'm a hit man.

It's all happened so fast, really. I'm looking now at the ring in my jewelry kit that all Black Hawks received my very first season. It's an expensive diamond ring Management presented us for winning the title our last year in the Eastern Division of the NHL. A wildly happy and most successful year in which we just nosed out the Bruins for the Prince of Wales trophy on the basis of more games won—even though we were tied in total points. The closest race in history.

The Hawks had been dead last the previous season, even with Bobby Hull scoring a record 58 goals. Then we'd started the new season dropping our first six games. Fans were singing "Bye Bye Billy" to Coach Billy Reay at the stadium, our own rink. And there were five round-eyed rookies on the squad including Cliff, myself and Tony Esposito, called Tony O.

Incredible is the only word to describe what happened. You could feel it starting to build, the whole team jelling, coming together as a unit, every single guy contributing something. The veterans bent over backwards to bring us new guys along, while we injected our almost boyish Rah! Rah! spirit into the team.

We kept inching up in the standings—into fifth, then fourth place. We hung there for a while, then suddenly we were third, building all the time. And before each game Billy Reay would come into the dressing room to look around in that penetrating way he has, chewing his gum hard, and saying those two things I'll never forget. If we'd been playing a string of good games, he'd caution us: "It's hard to live with success." And then before every game, just at ice-time, he'd clap his hands and say, "All right, fellas . . . tonight None Against!" This became our battle cry, one which I, a hard, corner-checking defenseman, took to heart immediately.

So every game, whenever a man would get loose in front of our net, I was determined there'd be no way he'd keep standing if I could reach him. He was taking money out of my pockets and pride from our team, as the phrase "None Against!" kept singing in my ears. Then we began calling it out together before each contest.

Soon we were in second place, just a few points from

11

first. And finally, number one. Fantastic! No team had ever moved from last place to the championship in one season. Along the way Tony O had accumulated a record 15 shutouts, was voted rookie-of-the-year and easily won the Vezina trophy that goes to the goalie of the team with the fewest goals-against average. He also won it this past season, when we anchored our second straight Western Division championship. "None Against!" all right.

I, too, received a distinction of sorts my first year: 213 minutes in the penalty box, the most in the league. And ever since, I've been considered a villain or a policeman, depending on where you sit. My second year I broke Howie Young's long-standing record of 273 penalty minutes with 291. This past year I finished with a sober and somewhat more sensible 199, eleven minutes behind Pittsburgh's obnoxious "Super Pest," Bryan Watson.

I've been engaged in more than a few scuffles during my three years up. But I'm not especially proud of them. And many of them, particularly those back in the beginning when everyone was trying to run me out of the league, were just plain dumb, the emotional tantrums of a child. I've had to smarten up a great deal. But I'd like to say *why* I fight, knowing as I do that not too many players are afraid of me and that I'm by no means the most effective fighter around.

I've often said that losing a fight doesn't bother me.

I've lost plenty, and I really mean this. But losing games does upset me. And playing and defending on a team that won't be pushed around is what winning—and my style of hockey—is all about.

A good player must do many things. He should skate with power and ease. And he needs to execute his stick-handling, his passing and his shot with lightning finesse. A defenseman must also develop his ability to check, a subtle maneuver designed to place the body directly in the path of an opponent at the optimum last split second. Crunch! The result is not intended to be subtle. Needless to say, we work on these points constantly.

But one thing you've got to have to be a success in this league can't be taught. Call it meanness, determination, desire or even, at times, stupidity. Yet whatever you label it, the ingredient is guts—and this means not being afraid of anyone.

My defense partner, Doug Jarrett, is called "Chairman of the Boards" for good reason. There's nobody who can hit quite like him. He just splatters guys, sometimes even two at a time. And that's a beautiful sight. Like homemade apple pie, my favorite dessert.

My own specialty is corner checking, a practice my Denver coach, Murray Armstrong, once told me was the "hot seat" of hockey. If you're good in the corners, he used to say, you'll be a good player. And nothing gives me greater satisfaction than going into the corner

with a player, bashing him against the boards, just laying him there as hard as I can.

One of my favorite plays is when the puck's free in
the corner. I'm coming from my position in front of the
net and he's racing down the alley for it. Everyone
knows we're about to meet like thunderclaps, to the
disadvantage of one of us. But it won't be me, I tell
myself.

So I get set, my knees locked and slightly bent, my
stance wide for good balance. My weight is forward
and I'm aiming for the biggest part of his body, eyes
riveted on the center of his chest. Then, at what I hope
is just the right moment, I hit him. If he wants to go
head-on, fine. And if I miss, hitting the boards myself,
that's okay too. The point is, he's not getting anywhere
near that puck. And, of course, I'm always watching
his stick. If it comes up, so does mine. If he raises his
elbows, mine go up there too. The greatest moment is
when he's tearing in, head down, and doesn't see me
coming at all. Then, looking down at him spread out on
the ice a little unhinged—that's nice.

Just as Billy Reay says, when you go into a corner,
leave them on the seat of their pants. Either there or
up against the glass so they'll know they've been hit.
And later you'll see them watching for you: worrying
more about getting you back or getting hit again themselves than about the game. Such a pop can also jack
up the spirits of your own team as well.

Of course, not everyone plays this way. Our own Billy White, for example, masters the corners by stealing the puck right off an opponent's stick. And Whitey Stapleton, who's a bit smaller, is of the rushing style, using his own net for a decoy and then quarterbacking the play all the way down ice. In fact, before "Mr. All-Time Everything," Bobby Orr, came along—a player the experts are still trying to categorize—Whitey held the record for most assists by a rear guard. He's still one of the great offensive defensemen in the game.

As for me, hitting may be doing it the hard way, but it's the only way I've ever learned—hitting, knocking an opponent off the puck, then trying to carry it out myself or getting it to someone else who can. That's all I know.

I first started pairing with Dougie Jarrett toward the end of my rookie year. Sometimes just before face-offs we'd glance at each other. "Bring on the Christians!" he'd call over while still wearing that bemused choir-boy expression of his, as I jerked my knees and took a few deep breaths the way I do before every face-off to pump up my oxygen.

When you stop to think about it, it's a violent, really almost pagan existence out there on the ice. No matter what your normal emotional structure is, you change. In fact, you must. Because suddenly you have no friends, no friends at all. Everything that happens is instant and unexpected. The puck, a six-ounce disk of vulcanized rubber, is one of the meanest missiles in

15

sport. And chivalry is dead—except for one or two cardinal rules like not slamming into a goalie outside his
crease and not hitting a man playing with a wired jaw.
But not even these are sacred, as "Little Joe" Sanderson
or John Ferguson will tell you.

When an opponent gets creamed, you're delighted.
No matter who did it on your team, you feel happy and
curiously revenged. Hockey is actually nothing but a
gutsy, brutal, brawling world, the roughest and least
forgiving sport. And it's easy to sense this blood lust on
the ice bringing the roaring crowds to their feet, which
in turn drives participants to even greater heights. It
just sends impulses racing up and down my spine.
There's something tribal about it, primitive really, a
little like what goes on among those jungle tribes of
New Guinea. Survival and supremacy are the keys, as
a number of us seem to regress into our brute natures.

I'm one of them. Perhaps all players are, deep down
inside. You just forget that hockey is a highly stylized,
time-honored sport with civilized traditions. Suddenly
you're back in the jungle; your voice is lower and less
articulate, like a mother bear protecting her cubs, growling that "no one's gonna push me out of here." Then,
still lower: "I've gained this much and I'm gonna gain
more."

The elders out there keep us honest, knowing from
their long experience exactly how much you can do.
And if we start to exceed our boundaries, start pushing

too far, they'll let us know with a glove in the face or a stick in the ribs. All hell can break loose—and frequently does. A violent testing for authority, with the veterans battling for leadership among themselves. Everyone's growling mayhem.

Three blind mice in stripes are trying to maintain control over thirty flaring tempers. You just can't tangle hard with someone several times a game and not become a little savage. There's no ethical master out there controlling it all, saying "Forgive each other." So, sure, "Bring on the Christians!" And to be truthful, I find it all deliciously exciting.

Maybe, however, it takes its toll. During my second All-Star appearance in 1971, the nine Black Hawks picked for the Western squad—essentially the same group that had beaten the cocky easterners 2–1 the year before on Bobby Hull and Chico Maki goals—flew to Bloomington, staying at the same hotel, eating our steaks together, sticking pretty close the way teammates will on the road. Of course, there's a little tension in the hotel lobby, where you're right next to Orr, the Mahovoliches, Park, and McKenzie—the fellows you've been knocking heads with all year and will be soon again. Things are a little cool, bits of conversation about trade rumors, that's about all. Because generally opponents tend to stay away from each other.

I saw the Boston guys and the New York guys, for instance, and didn't say hi. Hull was a charmer, of course, the way he always is. But to be honest, I don't think they like me much. Sometimes I catch them looking at me as if they thought I was a little crazy for fighting so much.

Anyway, in the midst of all this, something rather tragic occurred at our hotel. And it happened in the room right next to Pit Martin. A man climbed out of the window and Pit, who's a quiet and conscientious person, could see this fellow standing on the ledge, preparing to jump. But there was nothing Pit could do, no way he could stop him in time.

Pit, of course, was terribly shaken up as anyone would be. And all the players got together downstairs very solemn, trying to think of something helpful to say. Suddenly old Gump Worsley cut in with, "Well, the guy should have known better." He's got that very dry sense of humor, you know. So we all asked him what the guy should have known. "Well," replies Gump in an absolute deadpan, "he shoulda known that the pool is frozen over in wintertime."

No doubt about it. Playing hockey makes you somewhat insensitive.

And another thing. I've found that once you've played hockey, you tend to approach all games in a rough, aggressive manner. At least I do. Ask Cliff. We played lacrosse together back in Denver. Some of the first fights they'd ever had out there happened when we were playing. We'd cross-check with our sticks (a legal maneuver in lacrosse, but one we put a little extra something into) and even broke a few over visitors' helmets, which was seldom appreciated. Whenever an opponent sought to retaliate, Cliff and Craig Patrick, who now plays for the California Seals, would come in as a tandem and wipe him out. Most of this you can get away with in lacrosse, but it all came from hockey just the same. And all three of us midfielders were on the hockey team that Cliff captained to a record 28 straight wins and the NCAA championship that year. It was a lively lacrosse season, needless to say, despite my dislocated shoulder.

And today, when Cliff and I go back to Denver to work out before the Hawks training camp opens, we sometimes join in a pickup game of basketball with some of the college athletes. Pretty soon elbows are flying and guys are running at one another. Just a crazy free-for-all. Everyone's playing it loose, letting go, the way you can in hockey as in no other sport.

It was the same when I started night karate my last year at Denver. Each karate session would begin with the same traditional polite bowing ritual. In a fairly short time I reached yellow-brown belt, First Degree. But I never progressed any further, because my *cadas*—the different practice sequences you go through, which become more complex the higher your level—were not that good. I couldn't remember them all, so I lost on style points. Still I thoroughly enjoyed the free-fighting,

19

and I once heard the instructor tell someone that I had developed the most effective reverse kick he'd ever coached. (Those big Magnuson feet again; unfortunately, that's a move impossible to execute on skates.)

We'd have open competitions pitting the lesser degrees against the black-belt holders. It was understood that you controlled your punches and kicks to stop just before impact. But it didn't work that way. I wasn't overawed by the black-belters at all. In fact, I enjoyed testing them. And they knew it. You could see it in their eyes: "Man, this kid's got a lot of nerve! I'll show him." And sometimes our punches would contact—right on the nose, for instance. Then all controls would break down, and there'd be some real violence. Nothing phony about it; no Roller Derby scrap. Very much like a real hockey fight, in fact. True anger. And the funny thing was that just as often happens on the ice, everyone around us immediately stopped to watch.

My first three years in the NHL have been like this, too. A testing period. Just because a player has a tough reputation is no reason to be afraid of him. In fact, a hit man can't be afraid of anyone. Fear simply can't exist in your vocabulary. The only thing you ever think about twice is how tough someone else actually is, in order to be ready for him.

For three years players have been running at me to find out just how tough I really am. Perhaps they suspect I'm an easy mark. At times I've felt very much like a community punching bag. But things have been easing up a bit lately, perhaps because most people have come to realize that, win or lose, I'm here to stay. And no matter how often someone runs me, sooner or later I'll deliver as good as he gave.

By now I've been tested by just about every tester in the league, from seasoned veterans like Ferguson to such noisy rookies as chubby Rick Foley. It doesn't really matter how big a guy is, because a big guy can be dropped just as fast as a little guy. So I don't care much who the player is. If I can pick my spot, I'll go with him. And if I'm irritated enough, I'll even do the provoking. It's a fine line that dictates these things, an essential instinct that must be a part of every hit man's game.

There are many ways to play dirty, and most of these involve the stick—such vicious things as spearing and stabbing, for example. Or butt-ending, as it's called, when a player slides his glove down from the end of his stick just as he's going into the corner with someone and jams any part of his opponent's body that's open. It's dangerous—and it's also very difficult for a referee to spot. Gordie Howe, I understand, was a master at this.

I'll never forget my first real baptism as a rookie. Fittingly, it was on a Sunday early in the season. I'd already had a number of scuffles, of course, but these had been dance hall stuff—you know, a little push-and-shove, a few names—that never really got started. I was still finding it almost impossible to throw the first punch, a genuine reluctance stemming from my rigid religious upbringing. Also, in college hockey, there's hardly any fisticuffs at all. You drop your gloves in a college rink and you're automatically out of that game *and* the next.

Anyway, we were playing the Rangers in New York. Vic Hadfield, who's very tough and unpredictable, had been bugging me all game, but nothing really provoking. And here we were standing next to each other, nothing going on, the whistle blown, and out of the blue he just whips his stick across my mouth, good for six stitches inside. The incident caught me totally unaware. Since then I've never let my guard down, never taken anything for granted on the ice.

At college training camp in Denver we used to have mock battles among ourselves. The coach would blow his whistle and each of us would grab someone and pretend to fight with him. It seems that many of the fellows felt uncomfortable pairing off with me. Apparently, even playing, I'd get this terrible cast in my eyes. "The Look," they called it.

Of course, I never want to kill anyone. Fighting is just a way of sticking up for rights, both mine and my team's. And I'm dead set against dirty tactics that will seriously injure another player. I'm mean but not dirty mean, not vicious. Most of my penalties come from keeping my elbows high or roughing and charging, which are all body calls.

But one thing you'll never find me doing is intentionally using my stick. If anyone wants a stick duel, forget it. I may knock his stick to try to make him drop it—something that a few players, like Eddie "The Entertainer" Shack, refuse to do—but that's the end of it. Stick fighting is truly insane.

Those who live by the sword die by the sword. Boston's Teddy Green, whose long-standing reputation as a high-stick artist finally caught up with him, is just one example. But for me, it's just not worth it. I plan to be around this league for a long, long time, retaliating with my fists man to man. And that's all.

Wounds come back to a player, particularly when I'm standing in front of a mirror: "12 stitches owed Ferguson, 15 for you, Fleming . . . ," and so on. My mind returns to the incident. I recall when it happened and how. It's a practice, in fact, that helps psyche me up for a game.

Of course, when you do square off with a player, and each of you receives something, you generally call it quits right there. Things are even . . . for the moment anyway. But when only one person gets cut up, there's usually a carryover—a grudge remains. And eventually that latent hostility will surface.

It may take an entire season before that moment actually arrives: the right game, the proper situation, where a fight is necessary because your team needs something to shake them out of their torpor. This is what fighting should be all about. And there *he* is. That wound, that old debt, wells up like boiling water inside you.

Suddenly you forget there's been any waiting. Suddenly you're going to find out *right now!* Everything is hinging on the moment. And then instant gratification.

That's hockey. That's why you've been waiting, never forgetting, making sure that he's not forgetting either, worrying him, keeping his mind more on you than his game, reminding him of a primitive, promised rendezvous with fists for weapons. What better than the ancient form? And that's why, when you go into corners with the marked man, you must be ready for anything. Because he's tough too. He's been waiting just as you have.

People are always asking me about hockey fights. Some will come right out and ask, "What really happens in a fight?" "What's said?" "What starts it?" "Do you get hurt?" Others hedge around. But I know what's on their mind, and they know I know. Still, they seem to be uptight about the question.

But since fighting is a legitimate part of the game, I'm certainly not self-conscious about it. After all, the essence of a defenseman's game is to defend the net aggressively. In front of the net and in the corners are where a game is won. Opposing players enter my zone for only one purpose, to score goals. I'm there to stop them. So here are two forces that must collide, one to succeed while the other is frustrated. It's that simple.

I'm reminded of a few encounters with Montreal's John Ferguson—who I really do owe 12, right across the eyebrows. Oddly enough, he's already got a similar scar in the same place, which adds a kind of permanent scowl to his face. He didn't get it from me, however, and that's why I was sorry to see him retire last year.

But the main reason I miss Fergie is that I grew up genuinely admiring this tough, spirited player. And I still do. He was never a "homer"—a term we use to describe those exhibitionists who are reluctant to play rough except in front of a home crowd where their teammates will have to back them up once anything gets started. That's why some players in this league are actually scared to play in Boston. It's like walking into gangland. Fergie, however, was tough everywhere. And I try to be the same way.

I'll never forget my first game against Montreal. I'd been pegged as a scrapper, but it was still very early in the season and nobody really knew me. Then down the ice comes Big John Ferguson, and everyone's wondering, "What's the new kid going to do now?" And for a moment, so was I.

It was the second period, with the Hawks behind. A good spot to provoke some action. I made a run at Fergie from all the way across the rink, nailing him against the boards. Pretty obvious charging, I'll admit. The linesmen got between us fast. They knew Fergie would be on me in a flash. I did too, and I was extra ready. He's the kind of fighter who'll sneak-punch you. That is, line you up just right and suddenly blast. He'll never go straight on, which is one of my biggest weaknesses. Except I'm not a sneak puncher. I just can't hit a guy if he's turned sideways to me or hasn't got his dukes up.

Actually, nothing happened this time. There was a little pull-and-tug stuff as he tried to line me, but he never did. Then the referee was pointing me to the cooler. The crowd was going wild. Never had I received such an ovation. Hats and clothing and paper came pouring down on the ice. Everyone was standing when I reached the box. What a racket. I was shivering all over. "My God!" I said to myself. "This just has to be the greatest experience in my whole life."

What made things even nicer was that shortly after this happened we began slowing down the Frenchmen with our bodies, and we ended up winning the game. This often happens when a team is playing sluggishly, not moving, not being aggressive, not hitting. A fight just seems to inspire them, jolts them out of their complacency, and turns the game around. This is why almost every team has a couple of guys like me. And it's a good sight afterwards to see your own bench up and watching, and then to have Bobby Hull come over and whisper, "Way to go, Man o' War."

Confessions of a "Hit Man"

My next real encounter with Ferguson was the time he gave me my scowl. He checked me while I was bringing the puck out, and suddenly his stick slid up mine and cut me on the forehead. An accident. He was trying to knock my stick off the puck, and it was an obvious mistake. My hand shot to my head right away, of course. I was bleeding heavily. But what surprised me most was what Fergie did next. He apologized; he actually came right over and said, "I'm sorry."

Now that I think about it, I'd do the same thing if I accidently hurt a player, which is why I'll always respect John Ferguson. For years he was the muscular arm of that great old-guard Canadien spirit.

My last opportunity to have a go at Fergie, I turned down his challenge—the only time in my career I've ever had to decline. We were in the sixth game of the 1971 Stanley Cup finals in Montreal. We had led 2–0 in games, but now our edge had shrunk to a slim 3–2 margin. No team in history had ever won the Cup after dropping the first two games. But that statistic wasn't helping the Hawks much, as we were now behind in this one too.

Frankly, my own game was a little confused at this point. I'd not been able to play my usual hard-hitting style. Billy had told us all to watch it. He really needn't have. In crucial games you'll seldom see many stupid penalties. You simply can't take the risk.

In any event, we did have a man in the box on this

occasion when Ferguson hit me right in front of our net, immediately dropping his gloves and circling around me with his fists rotating in the air. "C'mon! C'mon! You little runt!" He was egging me, just taunting me into a penalty, exactly what Billy had told us to avoid. I can still remember my humiliation, fearing also that the team's spirit might flag. But I kept my gloves on.

We lost the game. And though I never question Billy, I shall always wonder how things might have turned out if I'd gone ahead with John. Billy himself thought it was a great move. When I got back to the bench he patted me on the back. "Smart hockey," he murmured in my ear. But deep inside myself a voice was crying out, "Magnuson! You lousy chicken!"

My most memorable real fight, I suppose, was the time I almost knocked out Philadelphia's Earl Heiskala, a mean 200-pound bruiser. This was during my second season, and Heiskala had received 171 minutes in penalties the year before—not too far behind me. But first a little background.

The previous summer I'd started working in the off-season as an account executive for the Joyce Seven-Up Company, dealing in promotion, handling new accounts and keeping present customers satisfied. Two nights a year now, Seven-Up throws a party for their distributors and van drivers in the Chicago area. Cocktails and steak before hopping aboard chartered buses to the stadium, where a bloc of seats has been reserved. Then back to the restaurant for pizza and what have come to be called the "Maggy Awards." These go to the achievers, and are presented by me.

The first "Maggy Night" turned out to be "Heiskala Night" as well. Two weeks before, in Philadelphia, he blind-sided me with a classic cheap shot—a stick on the side of the head. Then, as I was falling, he caught me with an elbow in the teeth. For a moment or two I was almost unconscious, and rising was no easy task. I stood there wobbly and dazed, then tried lunging for him. But the two refs were right there between us.

He said a few things, too, which were lost in the noise of the crowd. Quite naturally, I replied. But as he started to skate away I added, "Heiskala, you'll get yours!" And this I'm sure he heard clearly.

Nothing infuriates me more than this type of back-stabbing, something John "Pie Face" McKenzie and his teammate, Derek Sanderson, are pretty good at too. Heiskala is no longer around.

Lots of players do their "stuff" when I'm off the ice. Yet I still see it, because I monitor things pretty closely from the bench, and any cheap shot makes me just as angry as if it has been done to me. And if it's bad enough, I'll go after that player myself. Every policeman feels the same way.

In Vancouver Bobby Schmautz attacked our little Lou-Lou Angotti from behind. As Schmautz was skating to the penalty box I yelled at him, "You back-stabber! Why don't you pick on somebody your own size?" Actually, however, he's not really that big himself; about 5′ 9″ and 160 pounds, I think.

"Come on over!" he called, standing next to the box waving his arm. I was ready to come right off the bench after him, an automatic game misconduct that does no favors for your team, because you're out of the game. And with only four regular defensemen, this really puts a liability on the others. Louie says, "Shut up and sit down! I'll get him back myself." I've learned more from Lou-Lou than just about any other player. He's even-tempered, knows what he's talking about most of the time, and is a no-nonsense player. "Sit down, Mag!" So I sat down.

Anyway, before "Heiskala Night," all the Seven-Up people knew that Earl had something coming. "I owe that guy pretty badly," I'd told my boss, Bill O'Rourke, that afternoon.

"Keep your eyes open," he answered. Bill told everyone else to do the same thing. But still, no one could believe it when my first punch landed exactly seven seconds after the opening whistle. I was pretty surprised myself.

As it happened, Billy started Dougie and myself. Players are superstitious about a lot of things, and Billy, a scrappy little centerman once for the Montreal Canadiens, has many of these left today. (I wish I knew what he does at the racetrack.)

In games, though, he'll always start the same combination until we lose. Then he'll switch. This doesn't hold for goalies, of course. Just the five skaters. And he'll also wear the same suit against the same team. Nothing would change that habit. Except, perhaps, a losing streak. But the Hawks have never been involved in one since I've been with them, so I've never seen him do it.

Still, Billy had on his Philadelphia suit this night, and Dougie and I were starting as we had the last few games. Cliff was out there too, right opposite Heiskala on the wing. The face-off puck squirted down the boards on my side, and Earl and I raced for it, both knowing we were going to hit, both preparing for it. My feet were spread well apart, my balance was good . . . *oomff!* . . . I flattened him along the boards.

Right away he threw off his gloves. I wasn't exactly standing there myself. He tried to land the first punch. I ducked. I did exactly what Johnny Coulon had been trying to teach me. He's the boxer I've been taking lessons from since my rookie season.

Johnny always says, "Move! Strike! Then get back!" I moved, landed a right, grabbed Earl's jersey. I have large central knuckles. I could see him start to fade, eyes rolling back. Strike! He went down and just lay there.

I'd broken his mouth for a dozen stitches, as it turned out, and dislodged a tooth. Never before or since have I really injured a player this seriously in a fight. The

31

usual results are broken noses, shiners like the one Rosie Paiement gave Bobby Orr; and such minor cuts about the face as the ones Orr gave me. But this was considerably more, and did a lot to bolster my confidence as a fighter—though I was also a bit concerned.

People wonder if a player could lose complete control of himself, to such an extent that he might kill an opponent if he was able. I can only speak for myself. If a man goes down when I'm fighting him, I simply can't hit him again. If he wants to keep going, fine. But I'll drop it the moment he stops responding. By then he knows he's made a mistake, and that's all a good policeman is trying to prove. So that's where it ends for me. Anyone who can't exercise such controls on himself has to be a little sick in the head. But in any event, the law of mutual reprisals is just too strong for a player to run amok and not get nailed for it pretty fast.

I've been involved only once in a fight that was allowed to play out its natural course. Or so it seemed . . . just an eternity of hitting and, in the end, utter exhaustion. This was against Detroit's Nick Libett, a 10-year veteran and a pretty good match for me at 6′ 1″ and 180 pounds. We just kept going and going, and neither of us finished anything.

At first he was catching pieces of my face. He opened a scar, which is easily done, so I was bleeding freely. Newsmen and fans alike seem to equate winning a scrap with the amount of blood drawn. Outside of appearances, this isn't necessarily true at all. To me, blood doesn't mean anything. What counts is what you've done to the guy inside, what he'll be thinking about next time. With Libett, my mistake was not standing back and boxing him.

Most fights are so spontaneous that you're not aware of every move you make. In this case, however, I could actually feel myself weakening, softer and softer . . . hit, hit, hit . . . and finally each of us were just slapping each other.

Cliff was on the ice at the time and later told me that my eyes went glassy. Back home, I saw a replay of the action. Hard to believe. The two of us looked like marathon dancers, collapsing on each other.

But getting back to "Heiskala Night." The Seven-Up crowd was ecstatic. Just a few minutes after the fight, at 7:07 of the first period, I scored my first NHL goal, after playing for a year and never missing a game. I threw my gloves in the air—such an exuberant gesture that the Hawks have been kidding me about it ever since. You can guess what Seven-Up thought of that. I heard that one fellow said, "Jesus, Maggy's doing all this just for us!"

We won 7–1.

Shortly thereafter Lou-Lou Angotti gave me some practical advice. "Next time you meet Earl," he advised, "slam him into the boards and give him an elbow in the face, just to let him know you're around."

33

But I couldn't do that. Sure, I'd do it if he causes a situation like the last time. But I won't deliberately pick fights just for their own sake. I used to be somewhat of a bully when I was younger. That's over, however. Now I'll only go if I'm pushed and there's a job to be done. Otherwise I let things take their natural course. And more often than not, nothing happens. No fights at all.

When I next met Heiskala it was really quite sad. I checked him hard against the boards in my favorite corner and he didn't do anything. Nothing. All that fight in him had just died. The next year he went down to the minors, and I'm not even sure he's playing hockey anymore.

To survive in this world you've got to keep coming back. No one wins all the time. If you become intimidated, however, that's it. You'll never stick in the NHL.

I used to wonder what would happen if I ran up against a friend who'd been traded to another team. Cliff, for instance, or any of the Black Hawk regulars, my friends, the fellows I've been playing with ever since I came up.

One night we were playing the Rangers in New York. Wearing Number 3, I always sit on the bench between Number 4, Dougie Jarrett, and Number 2, Bill White, an easygoing, gentle sort of guy who psyches himself up for games just like a rookie. Bill can then suddenly turn not so gentle if he's pushed.

Anyway, Bill and New York's Ted Irvine were very

close friends during the years they both played for Los Angeles. Then, all at once, in the middle of a game, here's Irvine and Billy really going at it, punching like hell. Irvine landed the first one, and for just a split second it seemed as if Billy was thinking, "What the hell's going on?" before he too started swinging.

After the penalty I asked him, "What's wrong, Bill? I thought you two guys were buddies."

"Yeah," agreed Bill, "Teddy gets pretty fired up for games, you know." A remarkably charitable statement. I wondered what I would do.

Well, I soon had a chance to find out. We were in Oakland against the Seals, and two former teammates appeared wearing gold.

There was Gerry Pinder, a little bit cocky for my tastes, who'd become upset when Billy had benched him during the playoffs the year before. So he pulled the play-me-or-trade-me bit right in the heart of our drive for the Cup. "I'm no longer going to be part of the team," announced Pinder.

"He's got the wrong attitude," Billy replied.

It made big headlines, and the general public thought Gerry was showing a lot of guts—standing up against an injustice like that, particularly in view of losing all the playoff money. He needed it like an electric train set. His dad is one of the wealthiest men in Canada.

Paul Shmyr, however, had always been one of my favorite people on the squad. A real team sort of guy,

young and tough. But Paul was our "utility" defenseman and didn't get a great deal of ice-time. Still, he was
a helluva fighter. And despite his frustrations he was
always personable and cheerful, a genuine spark plug.

I remember one night down in the dressing room we
were all sitting in that funky, tense, pregame hush. We
were going up against a pacesetter, and things were a
little tight. Suddenly, Paul pipes up, "Will someone
please get a forklift? I'm going upstairs to collect my
fan mail." I can still hear the laughter.

So here it is, Oakland, with me and Shmyr and Pinder
all on the ice together. And Pinder had given me a
mean little sideswipe just after the buzzer ending a
period. He'd started skating away immediately because
he knew, I guess, that I'd be on him. As I turned, my
stick swung with the motion of my body and cut Gerry
above the eye. A rather stupid, accidental move. I low-
ered my head. "Maggy, what the hell did you do that
for?" I was thinking.

All of a sudden, here comes Paul. He's right on top
of me, gloves off. So off come mine and I grab his arms.
Next thing I know we're rolling around on the ice,
though not really trying to strike each other.

During our pregame practice session that morning,
I'd taken Paul's little boy, Larry, for a spin around the
rink on my shoulders.

"Well, see you tonight," I said to Paul as I left the ice.
I'm not one to say hello to friends on opposite teams

during pregame warm-ups or eye-ball pretty chicks sitting near the ice or sign autographs over the glass.
Maybe I'm just not that much of a pro yet. All I think
about is winning that game.

"Yeah. We'll see you, too," Paul said.

Later the same night, Cliff and I went out to eat with
our old college roommate on the Seals, Craig Patrick.
At dinner Craig leans across the table. "Say, Mag. Paul's
got a message for you."

"Okay . . . what is it?" I ask somewhat concerned.

"He says to tell Maggy there's no hard feelings."

"You tell him the same," I said.

I certainly don't hate NHL referees, even though
they have whistled more penalties on me in one year
than any player in history. Actually, I'm pretty good
friends with most of them, particularly the linesmen
who are always having to step between me and someone else in my less friendly moments. Frankly, I
wouldn't want the job. And the crap they have to put
up with—both from the fans and the players. You've got
to give them credit.

In the first place, they must be excellent skaters: up
with the play at all times, ducking pucks and perform-
ing acrobatics along the boards. And secondly, they
must be exceptionally strong, especially the linesmen,
because they get the living daylights pounded out of
them trying to stop all fights.

None Against!

One linesman, Pat "Red" Shetler—his red hair and mine has established a bond of sorts between us—is a comparatively little guy. I like the way he jumps right into the middle of the action. For some crazy reason, I think he appreciates my hotheadedness. Or maybe it's just that being redheads we empathize. But each time with Pat, it's a little drama. Dodging punches, he'll start saying things like "Maggy (or Red or even Keith)! . . . Cool it! . . . Now!" I can usually hear the words. "Hey Maggy!" . . . *crunch* . . . "Calm down!" . . . *pop* . . . "Or you'll get 10!"

Actually that 10-minute misconduct can come quite easily, particularly now with the third-man rule, which penalizes any third party who enters a fight in progress. It's good for the game, I'm sure. But it's also led to some outrageously cheap judgment calls. I hope it will be exercised a bit more uniformly in the future.

Swearing at the ref, of course, is supposedly an automatic Misconduct, but I've heard a lot of words and then seen nothing happen. Slam the door of the penalty box, however, and you're guaranteed one. Throwing your stick or slapping it down in disgust is another. And I agree, although I had to learn the hard way. It's simply stupid behavior. Billy had to threaten me with a $500 fine during an Oakland game for this kind of thing. He was absolutely correct. Quite apart from anything else, an M.C.—or, for that matter, any foolish penalty—

38

is an utterly selfish act that hurts the other members of your team.

Sometimes during a fight a head referee such as John Ashley or Bill Friday will skate over and yell, "Okay, you two guys! Stop this or you're out of the game!" This, of course, means a match misconduct, which carries with it an automatic stiff league fine. This one I usually hear.

But normally it's the linesman who reestablishes law and order. So here's "Red" again. "Maggy! You . . . can get . . . him . . . later!" And he'll grab me and start pulling or pushing me, trying to skate me away.

"Your team . . . they need you . . . here on the ice!" Yeah, I say to myself, he's right, they do need me here. And, just as fast, that momentary outburst of anger suddenly fades away. And I'm being skated around in a little circle by "Red," and he's telling me, "C'mon, you're ahead 3–2. You don't want to lose this game, do you?" Hell no! "Okay. . . . Fine." And we'll smile at each other.

Sometimes the two circles get a little close and you'll hear an unpleasant word or three from the fellow you were recently battling. But by that time it's over.

I'm often asked to rate referees on the basis of my frequent experience in the pen. Well, there's not a great deal of difference between them. They're human like the rest of us—with domestic squabbles, maybe a touch of the flu, and shirts coming back dirty from the laundry. They have good days and bad days like anyone.

39

And you've got to remember that they never win no matter what they do.

Yet each one has a few very distinct characteristics. John Ashley, for example, bugs me at times, and he knows it. After one game I said to him, "John, you know you're a terrible referee."

"Well, at least I'm consistent," he replied laughing.

John irritates me no end because I feel he more often calls me on my reputation than my play. I'm not Magnuson the hockey player, I'm Magnuson the penalty king. *Tweet!* No benefit of the doubt at all.

Of course, there are lots of "marked men" in the league who are whistled down for any number of things. Players love to take dives, for instance. These are Oscar-winning performances and look just like a trip. Oh! Oh! There's Magnuson again. Whistle for tripping.

Jerry "King Kong" Korab of the Hawks is another unfortunate because of his size. He's so big, in fact, that when he raises his elbows they're higher than anyone's head. Whistle, elbowing.

And it works the other way too. Players get away with murder against guys like Bobby Hull and Bobby Orr—hanging on, holding, tripping—almost anything goes. Officials may see these infractions but often don't call them, perhaps figuring that the best horses should have to carry a little extra weight.

So if I were to type these fellows, I'd say that Ashley

is the most unpredictable official before a game begins. You don't know how he's going to call the game until its under way. If he whistles a penalty right away, you know it's going to be one of those games where he's calling everything. But if he doesn't, you can plan to run at people all night. You just have to wait and see.

Bill Friday is a second type. He usually concentrates on the "bad guys" out there, which includes me. He watches every move we make.

Art Skov, on the other hand, is a bit of a crowd pleaser. He's good, but he also tends to get tied up in that democratic bag of "if I gave them one, then I must give you one. A trade-off."

There are others. But I'll let you work up the list. I'm sure I don't know how I would act in a referee's position. In fact, I've never even read the rule book cover to cover. That's an awful admission. But I do know that if I ever had the job I'd certainly try not to let a player's past affect my calls. On that point, I too would be consistent. But maybe I'd better stay with the linesmen.

You may wonder if my karate training has helped me any on the ice. Not much, to be honest. Certainly not the foot and leg stuff. I experimented with a few of the moves my rookie year and actually broke Carol Vadnais's nose out on the Coast. Come to think of it, that was the first NHL fight I clearly won.

But then I tried my karate tactics on Reggie Fleming. Funny thing, when I was still living at home just after

41

we'd moved to Saskatoon, we'd watch Hawk games on TV. Dad was a Chicago fan and this was just about the time that Hull and Reggie were breaking into the organization. Everyone knew my dad as "Big Swede," a tough man with huge fists. He'd sit in his armchair during the broadcasts, and whenever they'd be losing, he'd growl, "Great Scot! Get that Fleming back out there!"

My initial season, Fleming was out there all right, but this time in a Philadelphia uniform. And now it's me, the chippy rookie, who's trying to fill the very same role old Reggie had vacated a few years before. It didn't take long for us to get acquainted.

The game was still in the first period when Reggie and I collided. I began circling in my weird-looking and somewhat less than black-belt karate stance while Reggie landed four sharp ones on my face.

I don't know whether Dad saw this one or not, but trainer Skip Thayer was right there. And, as we headed to the dressing room for repairs, Skip took a close look at me. "Boy, you sort of took it on the chin."

"Whatta ya mean?" I said, glaring at him through my pretty well-battered face. "He didn't have me down."

That's one of my personal criteria—not beaten until down. But in a game the following year, when the entire benches of the Hawks and Bruins emptied on the rink and Bobby Orr personally bounced my head on the ice for a time, I had to change my values a little. Some called it the fight of the year, though for me it was simply a moral victory. I'd been down, but we'd won the game and I had scored my second NHL goal. Today, when I come to Skip for repairs, I still ask, "Who do you think won?"

"Who the hell do *you* think?" he answers. Then he adds, "Stop talking so much out there and land a few good first punches. It would sure make my job a lot easier."

I've got a high pain threshold. "You couldn't hurt that kid's head with an axe," Skip tells people. And I certainly needed that high threshold my rookie year, because I was taking stitches just about every game. I wasn't using my head much—"running ignorant" I call it today.

Again, my first season. Gordie Howe had been my child ideal. In my scrapbook I still have the picture of him I sent away for at the age of seven. "To my little friend Keith . . . Best always, Gordie."

Now as a new defenseman playing in Detroit I was not unaware of his reputation. He was a true elder of the tribe. And it's the elders who keep the juniors honest. At this, Gordie was Chief.

Tremendously strong, his shoulders came down to his stomach. Or, looked at differently, his shoulders began at his hips. Try to nail him coming down the boards; his head would be up and, besides, he'd be difficult to catch. Try to do anything else to him and he'd have something better waiting for you.

None Against!

I wasn't sorry to see Gordie retire. And I'm sure most players would agree.

Our second game against the Red Wings, I did somehow manage to bump-check him along the boards. But then, as I was leaving the ice after a shift, he slipped his stick right under my skates. It sent me sprawling, and of course the ref was down at the other end of the rink. He never saw it.

"You'll get yours!" I roared as usual.

He then circled by me and fired back, "I'll do it my way. You'll get the penalty."

It's a remark I'll never forget, because it told me so much about the way an old pro operates: holding back, not doing anything obvious. Of course, I'm now talking with more than 300 games behind me. But at the time I was just madder than hell.

So during our next Detroit outing I took him out from in front of our net, bodied him out of the way. Like Phil Esposito, he was at home in the slot, and he was strong enough to hold most defensemen off with one hand. Still I kept pestering him out front—not such a smart thing to do to a man who'd give you the end of his stick for an easy 12 as soon as look at you.

Then we began shoving. And suddenly here's Gordie and me grabbing each other. I can remember this: I was holding on pretty tight—right up around the neck, my body pressed against him, not wanting those arms to get loose—when he said something like, "Get off my

44

back you little fly!" And as the linesmen were trying to separate us, he reached across and rubbed his glove all over his "little friend's" face. A pretty insulting gesture. You can imagine how I felt.

At this moment, as I recall, he turned to Dougie with an unconcerned chuckle and said, "He's a tough kid, but he'll learn."

I received another bit of outside advice recently. It came from my brother Wayne, the musician, a band instructor who works with college and high school groups back home. Like myself, he's a perfectionist. He once told me that for him there's no greater experience than hearing a piece of music played while he conducts right in the center of it. He's drawing it all together, and for him nothing is more beautiful in this world.

Well, last year he wrote me saying that I was behaving like a martyr without a cause. And maybe that's what Gordie was trying to tell me too. See, I have been learning the last three years. You can't take everyone on at once, though I once tried. I started out playing like an untouchable. Everyone who hit me I had to fight—simply had to—because everyone was trying me out, and I frankly wasn't that good a hockey player.

But now, with experience, I'm beginning to feel it all come together like my brother's music. Such things as controlling the puck, knowing where everyone is on the ice—instead of returning blind into my own zone, head down, no idea of who's where—and making the right moves rather than running stupid all over the place—these happen more naturally. Plus playing my spot, knowing when to have a go at someone, how to time it right . . . and win.

Of course, I still yell at the team and play my special kind of raucous game. After all, I'm still Keith Magnuson. But now I'm learning to control it all in a somewhat more professional manner. And I'm sure that Wayne, and even Gordie Howe if he remembers me, would agree.

One last ironic note about advice. Back when I was five years old living in Wadena, a small northern prairie town of 500 people where my father ran a hardware store and everything was simple and direct, Dad had had his car fixed. When he found it was a lousy job, I went along with him back to the garage.

There were some difficulties, and I remember Dad bursting into that car shop office, reaching right over the counter with those long arms of his, grabbing the head mechanic by the shirt and picking him up straight off the floor. This was how arguments were sometimes settled where I grew up. Well, I was by his side, pulling on his coattails and crying, "Daddy, Daddy, please don't fight!"

Today, when Pop and Mom come to visit, there's Big Swede grabbing a hold on me and asking, "Keith, Keith, aren't you fighting just a little too much?"

CHAPTER **2**

Canadian Gothic

A person's toughness must come from somewhere, and in my case I believe it came from where I was born. Gothic, I learned in school, is something stark and unadorned, medieval, perhaps even primitive. My rural beginnings were somewhat like this.

Like every small town, Wadena has one main street. That's where Dad's hardware store was, not far from the post office and the Royal Canadian Mounted Police. Magnuson's Hardware was a big asphalt building. All glass in front with dishes and home appliances on one side and the nuts, bolts and screwdrivers on the other. The farmers got their supplies from us: nails, lumber, anything they needed. And they'd often buy on credit. Every once in a while, though, Dad would figure that someone had extended his credit too long and so he might go out and pay him a visit. But, generally, he was more than fair. He'd worked a farm himself, and knew the situation before harvest time. Still, when Dad moved to Saskatoon several years later, he was holding about $3000 in lost bills, which in rural western Canada is a small fortune.

But Dad had a generous heart: He'd fix flat tires on my bike, and in return he'd let me help him in the store. We had large nail bins in the back where I'd shovel bags full of nails for customers. Dad would then take the bag and weigh it and look down at me: "That's just fine, Keith." Seventh heaven.

This was also Black Foot and Cree country, a few of whom used to hang around town quite a bit. One, named Jack Sunshine because he always had a bit of a glow on, worked on the nearby reservation at a store that supplied the Indians. Once a trading post, today it's "an exchange."

Well, anyway, Jack Sunshine came into the store one day. He couldn't speak English very well and he always called Dad "Big Joe."

"Big Joe," he said, "Jack need money." Just like that. Of course Dad knew exactly what he was going to use the money for, and hated to see it wasted. But Dad took care of Jack anyway.

Just down the block from Magnuson's was the little grocery store where I used to buy candy. Right next to it was the railroad station where I saw Prime Minister Diefenbacker pass through. I was thrilled, of course, because I've always admired important people.

That was a great day for Dad, too. He adored the Prime Minister. The train came steaming into Wadena's station and the whole town, even Jack Sunshine, was out to greet him. There he was, standing on the rear platform waving and smiling—Prime Minister of Canada John Diefenbacker, the grasp of it! Dad even managed to get his wife's autograph, for me of course. He and the PM, both Baptists, were each from Prince Albert, Alberta, where Dad was once a guard in the penitentiary.

At bedtime Dad would tell me stories about the place. Like when he walked into a man's cell and found him hanging by the neck from a pipe. I was still very small and I used to dream about it all night. But the only real nightmares I ever had were about falling down some great distance or flunking out of school. Yet I'd always wake up or somehow survive. Odd how dreams work on you.

Still I kept asking Dad to tell me more prison stories. I wanted to know more about prisoners. And the subject remains fascinating even today. I wonder about Alcatraz, that deserted penitentiary out in San Francisco Bay. Has this anything to do with the very strong guilt feelings I get whenever I do something wrong? Probably not.

Our own house was on a pretty tree-lined street in the shadow of the church. I could get to the local rink by just running down a nearby alley that led to the high school. I'd have my skates on already and I'd run stumbling over the stones. Mother remembers me trying to skate at three. One man in town had a sharpener and would sharpen my skates for 50 cents. Only one sharpening job a year, however.

I'm very fussy about the condition of my skates now; and I'm always bugging Louie Varga, the Hawks' equipment manager, to doctor them for one thing or another. Just imagine, when I could only afford to have my skates done once a year. Unbelievable! Today I sometimes have them done between periods. Of course, I wasn't the only one. In a little place like Wadena there was never much money. And it's memories like this that keep a person close to the ground no matter what he does.

Uncle Mac, Dad's younger brother, ran the International Harvester outlet near the barber shop. There was a pool parlor behind the shop; and when Dad and I'd go to get haircuts, sometimes I'd sneak around the corner and watch. Dad didn't like this at all. The family code was no dancing, no movies, no gambling, no drinking or smoking . . . and no pool playing. Honor and obey. The whole works. And when anyone departed from the Holy Writ, my parents said he was "back-sliding." I suppose that watching pool, for me, was just the beginning.

But even Dad wasn't that strict a churchman. He'd tell other bedtime stories about some of his younger days with Uncle Mac when he strayed from religion.

From the beginning he always tried to plant the idea that Swedes were really tough. And, in fact, both he and Uncle Mac had terrible tempers.

So he'd set the scene. Usually the story would take place at night and involve some pretty good rumpuses when he and Uncle Mac took on everyone in the place, most often a hotel lobby or beverage room. Sometimes they'd even improvise rings for the occasion.

Uncle Mac was a drinker. Now I don't mean a drunk, but in Baptist language there are just two categories: drinkers and nondrinkers. You're a drinker if you drink anything at all, and Uncle Mac sometimes did. He was the wrestler on the team, the chief scrapper of the family, short and square and with the power of a bear. I once saw him pick a guy right off the floor with one hand. Feats of strength were important to him. He loved arm-twisting people because he never lost.

On Saturday nights all these farm boys would come in thinking they were much stronger than any "city fellas." Dad would describe how smoky it got in the beverage rooms, particularly in wintertime. All these people packed in, and Uncle Mac would arm-wrestle anyone. He also liked to pull fingers. He still likes to finger-pull with me today when I go home for a visit, and he almost pulls mine right out of the socket. Then he musses my hair and says, "Okay Junior, lets feel your muscles." His own are still fantastic.

Dad was the boxer, and no one beat Big Swede in the

ring. I always loved to playfight with him. Sometimes
he'd come home from work early and go a few rounds
with me, slapping me around just enough to show me
what to do with my hands. Today, even with one bad
leg, we still fool around back home. He'll just stand in
the center of the room, pivoting on his bad leg to meet
me. One of his open-hand slaps is just like a punch. I'm
usually on the floor before I know it. Like Uncle Mac
he still likes to arm-wrestle, and can take me at that as
well. He always believed that a father should stay
stronger than his sons. Neither Uncle Mac nor Dad
were hockey players.

Actually, I was a mistake, the product of a reunion
weekend where Mom and Dad had been married. I
guess Dad really got fired up. But I never felt resented,
although the unexpected fourth child did create a few
hardships for the family. My parents always went the
distance to show me I was wanted. Dad's way was to
rough-and-tumble me.

After story time, even if it was late, Mom would come
in and kiss me before I said my prayers with Dad.
Sometimes he'd linger to add, "Good night, sleep tight
. . . Don't let the bedbugs bite." I'd be lying with the
covers pulled up and just as he was leaving the room
I'd shout, "They won't bite me!" Then he'd grab my foot
or tickle me and this would start me laughing fit to kill.

In a small town everyone knows what's going on. My
brothers, 10 and 12 years older, were better in every-

thing than anyone else, which put more than a little pressure on me. Football, hockey, baseball, track and field, or even basketball—it didn't matter. Wadena itself was primarily Scandinavians. Dad is a full-blooded Swede and my mother, Birdie, is half-Swedish and half-Norwegian. When I was young we used to talk Swedish at home all the time. Now I can hardly remember a word of it.

The gossip in Wadena was pretty fierce. Everyone knew everyone, and I can remember this one family where the husband and wife were related and each of their children was deformed in some way—which really kept the tongues wagging around the winter fires.

This was particularly rough on Dad, who never allowed any real arguments in the store. No haggling there. Simply *whaap! Whap!* Argument settled. The Canadian Gothic approach.

When Dad returned to the church, abiding by its codes more strongly than ever, everyone expected him to settle down a bit. Which of course he didn't. And with his children, he was highly erratic: generous and kind one moment, harsh and vindictive the next, especially if one of us strayed from religion. Both my parents were convinced that if you didn't go by religion, you weren't going to make it in this world.

Of the four of us, Wayne was the most independent. This caused me some confusion as a child because I admired my brother and loved my parents. Yet Wayne was always rebelling in one way or another, and this ripped us all up inside. Wayne would really get some whippings, I'll tell you. And I was always running to Dad and saying, "Please, don't get mad anymore." And Dad's eyes would moisten. It was hurting him too.

And then I'd promise Mom that I would never be like Wayne, that I'd never disappoint Dad like this. Much later, when I began to drink at college, I knew I was letting them down and this bothered me at the time. Today, of course, they know I don't follow the religion the way I used to. But I'd never come right out and say: "You know, Mom, I just don't believe in some of those things." It would break their hearts.

I go to church at least once a month. It gives me a good feeling. And I accept notions like Heaven and Hell and living a decent life. I say prayers, believe that Jesus died for our sins, and hold to the Word of the Bible. But I also bargain with God just a little. This I began doing at a very early age.

My father puts religion before hockey. With me, it's the other way around. Naturally I want God on my side because He has the power to deliver talent or take it away. And being a good Christian is the best way to help my own performance in hockey. Quite possibly this is sinful reasoning. But before games today, I still find myself telling God that if we win I'll become a better Christian. Then later, when we have won and I go out for a beer with the team, I'll say, "If You're up there,

please don't strike me down." Whether I'm a hypocrite
or just human, I'm convinced that if God has been listening to me all this time, He's thinking, "Well, to Hell
with this guy." And so, whenever we lose a game, I'm
sure it's some form of punishment.

Of course, Wayne and Dad get along just fine now.
In fact the entire Magnuson family has pulled itself together at last. There's Dale the doctor out in Delta,
British Columbia, with his family. Wayne, the musician,
up in Foam Lake, Saskatchewan. And six children,
three apiece, all with red hair.

Then my sister Meridel, just a year older than me,
who's a secretary at the university in Saskatoon. She'll
occasionally come down to Chicago and we'll chat by
the hour. We're very close.

Mother is vivacious, artistic and outgoing, as well as
direct and uninhibited. Two years ago, when the Chicago press was criticizing the Black Hawks for their
Stanley Cup play, Mom sent them a letter of reproach
written on an air-sick bag during her flight back to
Saskatoon. She's the person to whom I'd confess any
wrongdoing, usually as I helped with the dishes. Then
she'd approach Dad. Now I let my secretary at Seven-
Up, Dolores Del Monaco, handle all touchy situations,
such as the lady who keeps calling to offer me $100 just
to shake hands with her son.

Dad has mellowed. At 65, he's doing well in insurance, selling mainly to farmers who love to see him be-

cause he has a keen awareness of their problems. He talks their language because his soul belongs to the land. One of his greatest pleasures, he tells me, is when he's introduced as "Big Joe Magnuson, father of Keith, the hockey player." Dad believes I'm a combination of the whole family: Dale's patience, Wayne's fire, Meridel's directness, Birdie's whimsy and his own stubborness. But regardless of whatever traits I've picked up as the youngest member of the family, I'll settle for being known as "Keith Magnuson, the hockey playing son of Big Joe."

Dad was once the deacon and choir leader at our little church. But when my brothers, particularly Wayne, began to slide, he resigned these posts because he no longer felt his family was under the Rule of God and, therefore, his usefulness to the parish was at an end. It must have been a terrible decision for him. Yet I've never been able to fault Wayne either. After all, he wasn't without his reasons. He once told me that when religion is forced upon someone, it can often cause a lot of hangups, and he wanted to think for himself more and to rely on his religion less.

I'm somewhere between today. Thinking for one's self is important, of course, but a strong faith can help each of us know what's truly right and wrong about our thoughts.

Each Sunday I went to church with Dad. We'd sing to beat the band. He was always right on key, with me some distance away but closing loud. Then when the sermon began I'd fall asleep in Dad's lap. At first he realized I was too young to understand anything the preacher was saying. But as I got older he would nudge me severely. That's when I began making up my lists of things to practice, jotting them down on the backs of sermon cards and pledge slips. As the seasons passed I did this for everything: baseball, swimming, basketball, track and field and, of course, hockey. I still have a few in my scrapbook, such as this one when I was 10.

"*Hockey.* 1. Skate right 2. Change pace 3. Turns for skating backwards 4. Ankle exercises 5. Turns-crossover and tight 6. Agility exercises 7. Stops and starts with weights 8. Changing direction 9. Figure eights 10. Skate backward 11. Stops backward and forward 12. Stick-handle: three ways—faking 13. One-hand carrying 14. Left-hand stick-handling 15. Passing: flat-flick-drop-back. . . .

And here's one describing a typical hour's workout:

1. Four times up and down the rink, stopping every four strides
2. 15 stops and starts
3. 2 times up and down rink hard
4. Skate backwards—do turns—try everything
5. Skate corners
6. Shoot—100 shots—10 shots from blue line . . . then stick-handle

7. Skate as many times around the rink till tired, alternating hard and easy
8. Time yourself for ½-mile
9. Skate around the rink carrying puck—head up
10. Zig-zag . . . slide glide . . . scoot . . . draw away . . .

Pretty ambitious for some 10-year-olds, but not in Canada. We all took our hockey seriously. And no one was ever more serious than I was even back then. Playing NHL hockey has always been the most compelling goal in my life.

At five I was playing organized hockey in Wadena's Tom Thumb League. It was intramural in that we had only one big squad. For any true outside competition, we had to travel quite a distance to such other small communities as Elfros, Winyard and Home Lake.

Whether playing hockey or not, I skated almost every night, tripping down the alley to the rink with my skates on. Townspeople of all ages would be out there playing crack-the-whip, and it really cracked if you were on the tail. Or we'd play roughhouse games of tag. Free-skating games like these are some of the best preliminary exercises for future hockey players. Ideally, you should be a good skater before you even grab a stick.

I began at defense because that's the position Wayne played, the same reason I was a catcher in baseball. Then, briefly, I switched to goalie. But that didn't last.

One night in Elfros, with me keeping net, their Tom Thumbers scored six goals against me. I cried all the way home and never stood in front of a cage again. Even today, when a goalie loses a game badly, I know how terrible he must feel.

I'm a bad loser. Fortunately, we didn't lose all that often. But when we did, I'd cry a lot and stay in a bad mood for hours.

After my brief goalie career I went back to right defense permanently. Wayne once saw me score two goals. Was I ever proud of myself! Right afterwards, I imagined myself a cross between Gordie Howe and Montreal's Doug Harvey. To make it even better, we produced a shutout.

"You played a good game, Keith," Wayne told me after the game. "But does your helmet still fit?"

"Whadda ya mean?"

"Don't get the 'big head,' " he said. "Don't ever think you've learned everything."

I've never forgotten that dialogue. In fact, it took me a couple of years to fully appreciate what Wayne meant: that a person must always try to improve at everything he does, and never think that he's learned it all. Probably the greatest single lesson of my entire life.

Sunday, of course, was The Sabbath, a day of rest. No activities of any kind, *including hockey*. My parents took it quite literally and would sleep all afternoon. And so I began slipping out to the rink while they rested. It took a few years for Dad to nail me. But one Monday he read in our paper that I'd scored two goals the day before. He was angry, of course, but he never punished me for it.

On the whole, however, I was a pretty well-behaved child. Through grade school I was an almost steady A student, thanks in large measure to a marvelous teacher named Anne Keele who really motivated me. "You're doing very well, Keith," she'd say. "But I know you can do even better." Her voice assured me that her remarks were intended for me alone, as if there was no one else in the class, and this got me working harder than ever. A few hockey coaches have this same gift. And later in life, I'd be fortunate to have two of them: Murray Armstrong and Billy Reay.

Anyway, Anne Keele was certainly among the strongest influences in my early years. She lived with her widowed mother and sister, Ethel, who taught me music. Frankly, I hated music lessons, because they conflicted with hockey practice. I'd skip them as often as possible to have just a little more time out on Wadena's winter ice.

My family all enjoyed music in one form or another, and we'd frequently sing together. I was the loud, toneless wonder in the group. But Dad had that big, rich voice. Mom and Meridel were decent sopranos. Dale played the piano and Wayne blew the trumpet.

About grade 7 I switched to trumpet. To be honest, I thought trumpet would be much easier than piano, with only one line of music to read. Wayne gave me a few starter lessons, but it was hopeless. I guess I just didn't have the interest. Finally I wrote off music altogether and absorbed myself in sports.

Not that I don't enjoy music today. I love to dance, though as Cliff will tell you I'm no Fred Astaire. We play records all the time—anything from light classics to contemporary rock, particularly the Big Soul sound, my favorite.

I'll never forget the end of my junior year at Denver when I was rooming with Cliff and Jimmy Wiste. Tschaikovsky's "Swan Lake" had been our theme song during exams. It was suitably dramatic music, and after we'd finished, we were all pretty punchy and just sitting around with a case of beer. "Swan Lake" was still playing in the background, of course. And suddenly, there's Wiste, a miniature Butkus on stubby legs, popping into the room dressed in a black ballet outfit—padded bra, frilly tutu and tights. He's way up on tip-toes, mincing around the room, fluttering his hands. Well, we almost died. But seriously, when I listen to good music of any kind, I can see Wayne's point about striving to achieve some sort of perfection. Because music is perhaps the most completely beautiful experience in the world.

Back for a moment, however, to those piano lessons at Ethel's. What made them even worse was that I had to take them with a guy named Kenny Doigt, a born pianist. His scales were always perfect and he'd whip right through them. Then old Ethel would turn to me. "Keith, let's hear yours." I was terrible. It would be intensely embarrassing and I'd just hang over the keyboard, burning up inside. Meanwhile, Kenny just sat there smiling.

One day, however, I enjoyed a brief advantage. We were heading for a lesson right after school and our route to Ethel's took us over the railroad tracks. A long, slow freight train was coming, just chugging along like a caterpillar. Except by now the warning light had started to blink. Kenny wasn't the daring type. He'd heard about people catching their feet and being flattened just a little. So he stopped dead while I ran across the tracks ahead of him, beating him to the lesson by twenty minutes. Of course my scales were rotten. Late or not, his were perfect.

I was pretty emotional, and certain things scared me quite easily. For instance, there used to be religious films shown at our church. Some were about Billy Graham or another great evangelist named Moody. These didn't bother me any. But then there were others set in Korea or maybe Japan where an American fighter pilot was shot down in the wilderness. His parachute would land near this village where the missionary was. And he'd accept Christ and be saved.

Or it might be a gang war with terrible fighting on

both sides, but one of the gang turns out to be a Christian and converts all the hoodlums to religion. None of this seemed phony at the time. In fact it upset me so that I'd either hide my head in Dad's lap or crawl under the pew.

I also cried easily, particularly over things that interfered with my hockey. Dad, for instance, used to supply me with sticks from his stock at the hardware store, but each one had to be pretty thoroughly whipped before I'd get a replacement. One day, however, he promised to deliver a new stick just before practice. He was a little late and by the time he arrived I was sitting beside the rink crying like mad.

We had a nice house—a two-story job surrounded in the spring by flower beds, purple lilacs and rich green hedges. There were also lots of plants inside, which Mom seemed able to grow just by looking at them. We had a big back yard with a trapeze set. And out front, right across from the church, stood a handsome elm sporting a giant swing.

In the basement was a water storage tank that filled whenever it rained. That's how we got our water. During dry spells there was a guy in town who filled it, but that cost some money, so we usually depended on the rain.

Our family had no flushing toilets. As soon as I was old enough, it became my job to carry the waste to the cesspool at the back of our property where the rats hung out. I hated facing those huge, well-fed, evil-look-ing animals that were always there.

Not that I had anything against animals. Our family always had pets. Once, in fact, I was down in the base-ment mopping up a leak when one of our cats decided to have her kittens on the top step of the cellar stairs. She was really yelling and suddenly, like my nightmares, one baby kitten fell straight down to the cement floor. I was sure it was dead, and I burst into tears. But my sleeping bag, directly under the stairs, had broken its fall. I carried this tiny, slimy little thing back up to the mother. She just licked it off. No problem.

But I was really shaken the day Dixie, our old re-triever, died. She was possibly the worst retriever in the world, useless in the field. Whenever Wayne and I went hunting, we'd try to borrow a neighbor's dog. But Dixie was a wonderful companion and exactly my age in peo-ple years.

Funny how dogs will show an intuition about things before they've happened. Just before we moved to Sas-katoon, Dixie came back home from her rounds one evening and died quietly under the elm near the swing. I took her in my arms out back and buried her, putting a little cross on the grave. I don't remember crying much. It was more all misty—that tearless, aching, em-pty feeling one gets after a true loss.

But there's a different side of animal life that's part of growing up in the country. When I was very young

Wayne would take me along on his trap-line expeditions. To keep in extra money, he'd trap muskrats and weasels and then sell their pelts. We'd bring them home and skin them in the basement. Sometimes, no matter how careful we'd be, we'd hit their smell pouch toward the back of the body and really stink up the house. That's when we'd really get it from Mom.

I wasn't older than six or seven when Wayne first put his mitts on me. I'd have to reach right inside the muskrat houses and weasel burrows where Wayne had set his snares. Often an animal caught by the leg or tail would just be waiting for me. They'd fight like hell. And, of course, I was terrified.

Wayne was an excellent trapper. One time, though, we had to chase this big mean weasel that had gotten away from us, into a culvert under the road. Wayne then sent me crawling through one end to drive the weasel toward him. Well, it was pretty scary, but it worked. The weasel tore out Wayne's end straight for his throat. He just picked it off midair like a goalie and broke its neck.

He kept a good many traps going all year round. Lots of people did this. It was just as much a part of western Canada as hockey, particularly in a small town where those few extra bucks were really needed.

Crows, for instance: You could get so much for a pair of legs. But there were restrictions as to where they could be shot. Otherwise, you'd be fined by a warden.

65

But that didn't stop Wayne. He'd pick them off telephone wires all the time. Once, I remember, we were driving along in Dad's car and Wayne had his pump-action shotgun in the back seat. Suddenly, here's this big fat crow sitting right on top of a pole. Wayne pulls over, reaches for the gun, and as he brings it up sharply to aim it bumps against the steering wheel. *Blaaaam!* He'd forgotten to put the safety on, and it blew the windshield right out. Boy, was I scared. And so was Wayne—but for another reason. He knew what Dad would do when he got home. And he was right.

Wayne seldom made such careless errors. He was a superior hunter who knew the flat, barren country around us like the back of his hand. He'd even arrange duck hunts for rich American sportsmen who'd come up and hire him as a guide. His job was to set the decoys and take the party to the area; then, while they were shooting, he'd wash their cars and make lots of extra tips. All this, of course, as a sideline while he was finishing school.

Sometimes he would set his traps on a farmer's land without asking permission. This was a common practice, but it made him a poacher just the same. Once there was a real showdown. Wayne had placed a trap near the road but still on the property of a guy named Lazar. We were moving it when Lazar caught us. "Get off my place," he roared, "or I'll call the Mounties." Wayne tried to explain that he wasn't hurting anything, not his livestock or his grain or his fields. And Wayne never did—never disturbed a thing. He tried to apologize. Lazar kept getting madder. Of course I hightailed it back to the car, anticipating the worst. But nothing ever came of it, though I do believe Wayne avoided Lazar's farm in the future.

Wayne's hunting and trapping made a huge contribution to our family. A couple of deer, for instance, would keep us in meat for the winter. I was practically raised on venison. And his ducks filled in the chinks beautifully.

The first time Wayne let me try his gun, I brought down two mallards with one shot. Beginner's luck. We'd gone early to one of his favorite places and before long, sure enough, here they came. And with Dixie gone I became the retriever. So there I was, splashing around these big sloughs, chasing half-wounded ducks. Why, a couple of times I paddled after them like a dog.

When I'd fetched them back to Wayne, he'd look at me and say, "Wring their necks!" But I didn't have it in me. Then Wayne, more the hunter, would do what he had to do.

There were hard lessons to be learned in the open prairies, he would tell me. And once when we were approaching a trap of his set alongside a stone wall, we saw a weasel in the snare still very much alive. It had been there for a day and a half at least, and the weasel was trying to gnaw off its own leg. This poor creature—

long, thin, brown in summer, all white now in the bitter cold of winter—being driven to such extremes by its simple will to survive.

Our springtime was always muddy. Huge ponds of meltwater appeared in the low spots. Sometimes we'd build rafts to explore these, and just as often they'd suddenly fall apart, plunging us in way over our heads. Once when I was wearing heavy boots, I came damned close to drowning.

June and July were the really hot months. Temperatures up around 100. Never much humidity, but such dry heat it would suck the moisture right off your face. And when we walked through the underbrush there'd be a crackling sound. Summers, of course, were pretty active in the extracurricular department. For me, no music lessons. For my brothers, a chance to make some odd-job money.

This one year, Dale was home on vacation from college and Wayne was about to be a freshman. Dad was determined that all his sons finish school before they did anything else in life. Well, my brothers together with another friend had been hired to paint this farmer's huge barn. I tagged along as "helper," and before the job was over, we'd all fallen off that barn maybe 15 times. No harm done. Early on in this project, however, Wayne began developing this thing with regard to a large Shetland pony pastured nearby. He was determined to ride it. Every day he kept trying to mount that stubborn old beast, and every day he was sent sprawling in the hot prairie dust. Nature's revenge.

We split about $150 for the job, or were supposed to at any rate. But Dale needed the money for college. And Wayne bought a new gun. So when it came to me, I didn't get a thing. But I didn't mind. I probably hadn't helped much anyway. Besides, the summer had been worth it just to see Wayne try to ride the Shetland.

And then, of course, there were our Canadian winters, extending from September to April with temperatures as much as 30 degrees below zero for weeks at a time. Each snowfall would add just another layer to the ground. It would never snow and then go away, or be cold and then warm up like it does in Chicago. Instead, it would stay bitter cold for months.

I was once out with a group of boys when everyone back in town thought we were frozen dead on the prairie. Actually, we'd simply skied out to try some sand dunes for a few hours. We didn't realize how cold it was getting, until we noticed that our feet and noses and ears had begun to freeze. Ironically, Wadena's only Lone Star Scout was with us, the highest honor you can get in that program. He was about 14, and we all called him "The Lone Hope." When you're that high, you're pretty much alone all right. Anyhow, The Lone Hope wasn't much help this time. We just barely made Wadena. And my cousin Dwight had to be pulled in on a toboggan. Some ski.

But we sure had good skating. The rinks, of course, were out of doors. And when it snowed a lot, we'd shovel all day to play an hour. Then it would often snow all that night, and we'd be back shoveling all the next day too.

The experience of small-town life, so close to the basics, is foreign to most kids. But this kind of background has helped many Canadians like me to realize exactly where we are today. And it has helped us as well to develop a certain toughness of attitude that we can draw on while out there on the ice. Without it, I wonder how many of us would be playing in the NHL today.

The day I left Wadena for Saskatoon, one of my best friends told me I'd soon be a big-city slicker. I doubt it. The last time I visited Wayne on his little farm, we were out in the pasture seeing who could hit a softball the farthest. Well, I hit a fairly long one and Wayne marked it off. Then it was his turn, and he really powdered it. Here I am going back, back, back in the pasture trying to get under it. The ball was still sailing when I stumbled over an enormous cow flop. Of course, when I look up, there's Wayne laughing himself sick. No contest. But next time, Wayne. Next time . . .

CHAPTER 3

Saskatoon

I never wanted to live in the city. But Dad got such an excellent job offer to go with a hardware wholesale company in Saskatoon that there really wasn't any choice in the matter.

Saskatoon, at least by my standards, was enormous— a city of approximately 115,000 people located in the central Saskatchewan prairie and about 200 times bigger than Wadena. I was sure we'd no longer know our neighbors, in the small-town way. I mean really know them. And, anyway, Saskatoon was where my Wadena friend had told me I was going to soften.

Actually, about the only real change for me besides my advancement in sports and dropping music lessons was that I began calling Dad "Pop." Well, not entirely true. Because there was also one other change.

Back in Wadena I'd earned myself a reputation as

something of a bully. I'm not quite sure why. Perhaps it was just knowing that I had big-shot brothers and a pretty fierce father in the same town. But I could also be quite easily goaded into arguments. And because I was big when I was little, I'd usually beat up my peers.

Of course, it didn't get me anywhere. Sure, at the time I might win a point. But then I began to realize that kids didn't want to play with me. This hurt. And I began to feel somewhat of an "outsider"—very much a loner except when I was with Wayne.

So to try and get back inside, I resolved to change my act. I stopped pushing other kids around. I'd hate to think that the fact they were catching up to me in size had anything to do with it. The truth is, I really wanted friends. I'd simply have to channel my volatile temperament into other sporting accomplishments. And as the challenge was achieved, recognition began to come.

All these things were beginning to work out just about the time I hit my new school, Churchill Elementary, in Saskatoon. Here I planned to make friends with everybody. So the first day I'm out at recess, the new kid with patches on his knees and not a dime in his pocket. This is fourth grade and all my Saskatoon classmates are dressed in these sharp-looking clothes and they've got new plastic yo-yos, the little extras I didn't have. And here they are choosing up sides for a football game.

One of the captains was a big heavy kid who's still a

pretty good friend of mine today. But at the time he just looks at me and says, "We don't want any of you farm boys."

There was no way I could take this, yet I didn't want Wadena all over again. Actually, it was a bit like a hockey game: You don't go looking for enemies, but you can't afford to be pushed around either. The kid was pushing me too far, I decided.

Just then Tim Gould stepped forward, an easy-going and likeable boy who was to be my closest friend right through college. Tim, who didn't know me at all at this point, says, "Well, I think he can play."

The fat guy isn't listening, however. He starts to lean on me, pushing me around. And I just exploded. I punched him to the ground, putting my hands around his neck. "Do you give?" I kept saying. I was shaking all over, almost crying with emotion. I can still get that way today. And I was also a little frightened with all those strange kids around, and me with their friend on the ground. Anyway, he gave pretty fast.

That was about all there was to the incident. But the results were interesting. From that moment on I was accepted. No one really tried to challenge me after that. And, I might add, I've never been considered a bully since—except, perhaps, in Boston.

Tim and I quickly became inseparable friends. I was over at his house all the time having sandwiches or meals. And once in a while I'd even play card games like canasta—very much against my religion. I also went to drive-in movies with his family—more sliding. But Pop didn't mind too much as long as it was something like a Walt Disney and I kept up my Sunday night church attendance, though sometimes I'd even stay home from church to watch "Bonanza." I hated to tell him things like this, however, so I'd leave my diary open in a conspicuous place with a note beginning, "Sorry, Pop . . ." He never said anything, possibly because my parents believe that if you admit your mistakes, God will forgive you.

By now, of course, both my brothers were well along in college. Wayne was attending the University of Saskatchewan in Saskatoon and supervising the local outdoor rink on our block. The rink belonged to my school, and they paid Wayne a salary for looking after it at night. Great for me.

Saskatoon had lots of teams and strong leagues for all age groups. Tim and I were Pee Wee defense partners from the outset. And this pairing lasted right on through college, a total of 13 years. We made a mighty effective tandem and always ended up on the championship team no matter what level we were playing. I was primarily the checker; he was more the puck handler. Needless to say, we came to know each other's moves blindfolded.

It was the same in everything, any little old pickup game; Tim and I always played together. In football I was the quarterback, hardly able to see over the line, but out there playing end would be Tim, big enough to muscle down my passes for a touchdown.

And I'll never forget one of our championship baseball games—Magnuson catching, Gould at third base—when someone stole third on me. I had terrible control. My throws were always too low or too high. But this time I threw the ball way over Tim's head.

His dad, who was coaching our team, got pretty excited. And he comes running toward me yelling, "Maggy! If you can't throw the ball, then don't play this game." I was almost crying when Tim comes rushing in from third base. "Shut up, Dad! He's trying his best."

In sixth grade, believe it or not, I won the Most Gentlemanly Hockey Player award. Just across town the same year, a player named Cliff Koroll was winning the same honor at Princess Alexandra Elementary. And I remember him then: His ears stuck way out from his helmet.

In seventh and eighth grades I had private hopes of being selected for the Pee Wee All-Star game. When I wasn't, it really shattered my pride. Tim was picked instead, and we talked about it frankly so that our friendship wouldn't be hurt in any way.

Tim always encouraged me when I needed it most. Going into high school, I was still only about 5′ 6″ and 140 pounds. I wasn't a fast skater. And as for my shot, well, the seniors used to yell at me, "Give it up! You can't even reach the net from the blue-line!" And there would be Tim, just chuckling: "Don't worry, Maggy. You'll make it." And together, Tim and I were named to the Midget All-Stars later that same season.

Every summer from the age of 12 on, I'd work at the Boychuck Lumber Yard from the moment school got out in the summer until it began again. I'd cut two-by-fours or load 80-pound cement bags, and go out on deliveries or work construction projects such as building a grainery. At the end of the day it would also be my job to collect the scrap and throw it into a big burner. My third summer I received a princely raise: $1.50 to $1.75 an hour. I was mighty pleased at the time.

The job taught me to work hard. Yet every night, no matter how tired I was, I put myself through a full workout, including a complete barbell program together with my normal calisthenics. Sometimes Pop would help me when I couldn't get a weight up the first time.

Finally came that magic summer when I was 14. I grew four inches, and my weight rose to over 160. Unbelievable. Now, as I confided to Tim, I was really ready to make it.

Like every promising young hockey prospect in Canada at the time, I became part of a truly organized series of teams and leagues. Starting with Tom Thumbs, on through Pee Wees, Midgets, Juveniles, all the way to the lofty Junior bracket, where the chances were that some professional club had their name on you.

Most of the teams we played for were sponsored by some pro organization. And, in effect, this arrangement bound you to that particular pro team should you decide to venture into the professional game at any time in the future. For most young players, however, the only real question was whether or not they were good enough.

All my junior hockey in Saskatoon was played for clubs—the Kingsmen Pee Wee Organizers, the Midget Red Wings—sponsored by the Los Angeles Blades, now the Kings. I was Blades property at 10 years old. By the time I'd reached 16, however, Chicago and L.A. had worked a deal transferring Cliff Koroll and me to the Black Hawks while sending Howie Young and another player to the coast.

Well, that's life. It's like being a product on the exchange—a negotiable item among high-powered businessmen. Even at 12, I recall having to sign a professional sponsor's form stating that in the event of injury or disablement they would not be responsible. Sure, fine, where do I sign? Of course, my parents had to co-sign as well.

Something more about junior hockey: The senior year in high school marks the exalted Junior level. This is where the competitive crunch comes to bear, as it's this plateau that supplies practically all the players in the NHL. First, however, you have to be invited to try out for a Junior team. And if you make it, you're in for an incredible schedule of games. All junior teammates go to the same high school and board together. But the sad fact is that many of them don't finish school at all. They get so involved in hockey that they neglect their studies and become "hockey drop-outs."

Consequently, it's a pretty big gamble, because not every junior makes big-time hockey. And if he doesn't, he has no education to fall back on. This has ruined more than a few young kids, and it also explains why there are only about 15 college diplomas playing in the NHL. I might have been ruined, too, if it hadn't been for Pop.

Still, you can imagine my pride the day the letter arrived from George Agar, coach of the Saskatoon Junior Blades, inviting me to come to their training camp. This was the big-time, the ultimate echelon in amateur hockey, the seedbed for the NHL.

Part of Agar's letter promised: "The schedule we have this year, I think, will work in with schooling as most of our road games are on weekends." Boy! What a laugh. My last year in high school, while playing with the Blades, I missed over half my classes and was flunking right up to final exams. The whole winter was nothing but hockey. And my parents weren't too happy about that, I can tell you.

There were a few side effects too. Such as the night I

received a head cut from a skate that grazed the corner of my eye and required 40 stitches. I can vividly recall being laid out in the training room. They thought I was unconscious, but I could hear them talking in hushed, worried tones about calling in a specialist. Pretty scary hearing these things for the first time.

Then they did the sewing without an anesthetic. A really weird experience—not a steady pain, but a lot like when you have your teeth drilled and the dentist hits a nerve, and then he does so again and again. That kind of pain. You can see the hooked suture coming down near your eye. Hear the crunch of the needle penetrating your flesh. I never have gotten completely used to stitches. When Mom saw me later that night, my head half-covered by a thick compressing bandage, she almost died. And before the winter was over so did Pop, but for another reason.

Late in the season Murray Armstrong, Denver University's coach, made his annual scouting visit to Saskatoon, where he watched the Blades perform in a playoff game. Cliff, a year ahead of me, was already at Denver on a full athletic scholarship. After watching us play, here's Murray offering scholarships to Tim and me, as well as Bob Sutcliffe, Don Theissen, Dale Zeeman and Neil McQueen. The six of us had also been Midgets together. Precisely the same six. Incredible.

The trouble was my grades. No, I guess it was first my parents, then my grades. The family wanted to see me in college, of course, but preferably one where I could live at home like Wayne. Pop felt it was against God's will to split up a family unnecessarily. And the only time I'd ever left home before was one summer when I was supposed to go to Bible Camp for a week. Well, I got so homesick that Pop had to come pick me up. So I didn't have much of a track record.

But Murray visited my folks, came right over to the house and sat down with them. Pop remembers him saying, "Look Mr. and Mrs. Magnuson, I'll take care of Keith," because only then did they agree to let me go away. And the funny thing was that Murray did indeed take care of me. Almost to the point of being a second father.

But still there were my grades. All through school up to this year, I'd never had anything lower than a B average. Suddenly, here I was flunking everything cold. Senior year, however, a student's final grade depends entirely on an exam issued by the Province to everyone in the twelfth grade. I'd missed well over half of my 160 school days, yet with two weeks to go until exam time I still had one last opportunity to pull my record out of the fire. No one appreciated this more than Pop. And during those last two weeks he wouldn't let me leave the house. Net result: a B average on my exams. And because the academic rating of Canadian high school curricula is so much higher than the States, this gave me the added bonus of 40 college credits at Denver before I even arrived.

I often think back to that little outdoor rink in Saskatoon, the one Wayne supervised at night. It would be late—maybe 10:30 or 11—and everyone else had gone home to bed. Wayne would give me the keys to lock up the warming shack—just a single room with a stove and a record player for skater's music.

He'd tell me to shut off the lights first, otherwise people might wonder what was going on and call the police. Then I'd be alone in the dark to do my exercises under the stars. I'd go though my stick-handling, shooting, passing and general skating routine no matter how cold or windy the night.

How I loved it. And sometimes, resting between exercises alongside the rink, I'd listen to the quiet and look up at the stars. For the moment it was just between me and them, like sharing a secret. And that secret, which was slowly beginning to reveal itself, was that someday—one day—I'd be playing in the NHL.

CHAPTER 4

Murray, Denver and Dawn

Everything happened so fast in that last year of high school that I've probably made it sound rather easy. Not so. Besides hitting those Provincial exams convincingly, there were letters of recommendation to scramble for, forms to complete, physical examinations to get. And to top it off, I was not finally accepted at Denver until about a week before the fall semester actually began. Until then I was one worried kid.

I hadn't applied to any other college, not even the university next door. And with time running short, I began to picture myself devoting an entire lifetime to the Junior A circuit—or even the slightly less accomplished Junior B, where your eligibility runs out at age 21.

By now I was Black Hawk property and destined to

be sent to one of their farm clubs in the Central, Western or American leagues. I wonder what affect this would have had on my career, whether it might have altered the feeling of momentum building inside me. I've known quite a few talented young players who got lost in the shuffle like this. Today several are playing in Canada's Senior League for beer money, which is like being a hockey bum. And when they finally come home, they're glad to get work on golf courses or as city help on the streets. That's rough. So there's no question but Denver was a key stepping-stone in my life.

That's why I strongly believe that all young people should go to college. If hockey will pay your way, so much the better. If you're good enough to go on with the pro game afterwards, you'll know it when the scouts start coming around. And if they don't, at least you've got yourself an education.

Once it was said that if you weren't in the NHL by 21, you were through. Of course this isn't true anymore, to which Cliff, Lou-Lou Angotti, Tony Esposito and Ken Dryden will attest, among others. Cliff says there's a trend in society today to appreciate the long-range benefits of an education: then you can get a good job and live a good life long after sports are over. And at Denver, Murray Armstrong would always stress education over hockey, ". . . with as good a set of grades as possible."

83

None Against!

Frankly, I'm not sure I heard this last part—maybe because I've never put anything ahead of hockey. I was mainly interested in just holding the C average a player needed to stay eligible for college competition. My studies suffered, but in their place I learned something about taking responsibility. And I began to understand the meaning of certain concepts: heading a family, planning an estate, managing my own affairs, as well as little things like how to eat right and when to take my pills. Of course, you don't really see it this way when you're a freshman.

Five Saskatooners roomed together their freshman year: Bob Sutcliffe, Neil McQueen, Dale Zeeman, Tim Gould and myself. None of us had ever spent much time away from our families before. But now I find it incredible how naive I was, even compared to my roommates. I had to be about the squarest individual on earth.

For one thing, I'd never had a drink before coming to Denver, and I continued to abstain all the way through that first college year. At high school, of course, guys were always trying to get me to do bad things, such as drink beer. But I simply said no. Religious conviction was part of it, but the rest was just not wanting to do anything that would hurt my hockey, fearing that God might take away my abilities. It was the same at Denver.

My first night there, in fact, I went out with a group

When you're alone in a corner, it's best to brace yourself.

The Toneless Wonder performs under the elbow of brother Dale. Sister Meridel is at the piano.

Gail was my only girl through grade 12.

We were the Midget Provincial champions in 1959. I suspect you'll be able to find me.

Cliff Koroll, me, Jeff Jehnings, and Jimmy Wiste—Denver's fearsome foursome. Cliff and Jimmy were co-captains my junior year, the same year we won the NCAA title.

From behind my legs look a bit bowed.

This time my protagonist is Montreal's great Jean Beliveau.

— *Wide World*

Rosa Lee, an amateur artist and Black Hawks' fan, painted this portrait of me from a photograph taken shortly after the Canadiens beat us four games to three in the 1971 Stanley Cup finals.

of players to a bar and ordered milk. Everyone cracked up. They just couldn't believe it. And from whom would I receive reinforcement now? I felt lonelier than ever. Right then I decided that hockey was going to have to take over. I'd attend to my scholarship as well as pin-money jobs such as hashing at sororities and caddying on the golf course; but otherwise I'd pour myself out on the ice. On the betterment side, I joined a Baptist youth group and went to church every Sunday.

About girls. I'd never believed in dating much. To be honest, I was afraid it would hurt my sports. Actually, the first injury I ever received on skates was back in Wadena when I smashed into a girl playing tag and broke my arm. From then on I was truly convinced that girls and sports don't mix.

Tim began dating Faye Youngren back in eighth grade; they got married when he was still in college. Early on, he was the most talented hockey player I knew. But then he began to lose a little of his competitive edge. His involvement with Faye split his thinking. Nights when I was out skating, he'd be taking Faye to a show. After college he bounced around the minors in Rochester for a while, but today he's not in hockey at all. Not that he's unhappy. He and Faye own four sections of land back in Saskatchewan and plan to do some farming. Yet I still have the impression Tim's not quite as happy as he might be if he'd made it all the way in hockey. At least that's what his old buddy thinks.

85

None Against!

But there were other girl problems, too. I'd been taught that there was only one kind of girl—meaning a true Christian like myself, of course. A Baptist. I'd witnessed my parents when Wayne started running around with a Catholic in high school. Naturally, this was against God's will, they felt. And again quite naturally, I believed them. Until I met Dawn McDonald.

Five young Canadians living together away from home led to some pretty wild times, particularly since we were rather more athletically than scholastically inclined. In fact, our pad was the campus noise center. That we pranked back and forth goes without saying, and more often than not I was the fall guy. You wouldn't believe how gullible I was. Or, perhaps, stupid is the word. And I still am today—gullible that is.

One night I walked in from my hashing job to find Sutcliffe sitting there, looking very solemn. Sut was about 5′ 8″, 190 pounds, with an incredible build, like a trash barrel. He'd never lifted a weight in his life. Just a natural mesomorph. The trouble was that all these muscles made his skating a little stiff-legged. But I digress. So I ask him, "What's the matter?"

"We've just kicked Neil out of the room," he answers.

Now, there's no reason not to believe him. McQueen was always a bit of a loner, and rather tight-fisted as well. So we didn't love him a whole lot, and let him know this from time to time.

Anyway, I checked around and sure enough, all his

clothes are gone, his books and everything. "Great Scot! He really *is* gone," I said. Sut just sat there brooding and nodded.

What had actually happened, of course, is that Neil hadn't gone anywhere. Sut, Neil and the others had simply moved his stuff into a friend's room down the hall. It was all an elaborate hoax just for me. So meanwhile, I'm busy explaining to everybody that we really shouldn't be doing this no matter how we felt. Neil was a long way from home. Where was he going to stay? Maybe if we just laid it on the line to him, he'd shape up. It was quite a sermon, to which everyone just shook their heads glumly. "Sorry, Maggy, we've made up our minds," said Sutcliffe. And they all left.

I'm pretty upset. A few hours pass, then another friend appears who's not in on the joke. He asks me what's this moving about, Neil going down the hall and all. Suddenly bells rang for me. I told him we'd kicked Neil out and I was about to call his parents back in Canada. Then I left a note on the table for the others, saying I'd just had a long talk with Mr. and Mrs. McQueen and they wanted to hear from their son immediately.

Boy, when I returned after a long walk the guys were sweating bullets. A call home was the last thing in the world they'd expected, especially Neil—who by this time was back. "What'd you tell 'em?" everyone kept asking. "What did you say?" They were obviously shaken.

Interestingly, Neil's attitude picked up remarkably. And I even began to laugh at myself a bit.

Because of hockey, my classes were all in the morning. And though Tim and I had both wanted to major in Physical Education, we didn't because their sessions were usually in the afternoon. Murray, our guide, then suggested Business, knowing that whatever we learned would always be a help to us.

So Business it was, and the first year we had to take all the basic requirements: accounting, real estate and business law, together with some required general education courses like psychology, American government and math. Also one I'll never forget: Arts & Ideas.

Arts & Ideas was taught largely in the dark from slides of ancient Roman buildings, armless Greek statues and the Pyramids. Quite a few hockey players seemed to take it because of the excellent rapping opportunities the course provided. Of course, occasionally our lady instructor, who to be honest was rather ponderous, would suddenly flick on the lights. And at this point some of us were faced with having to make dramatic returns from vast distances.

I had plenty of trouble staying awake. There was one particularly difficult Business Law course taught by a Professor Johnson, a lawyer who knew Murray pretty well. His class was almost impossible. And he was very strict as well. Three strikes and you were out. Literally.

I can certainly remember the first strike. My sleeping head was in the lap of a girl next to me whom I didn't even know at the time. Dawn McDonald.

"Magnuson!" I shot to my feet in one motion. "You're a jock, aren't you?" He knew the answer.

"Yessir!" I answered, standing at attention. Believe me, I was scared stiff-legged.

"When people fall asleep in my classroom," Johnson went on, "it tells me something. *That they're not interested!* Is that your problem, Magnuson?"

"I'm sorry, sir," I murmured, red as I could be.

After class, however, I spoke to Dawn for the first time. What a way to be introduced! We'd laugh about it after that, but I didn't really begin seeing her until my second year when we were living in the same "corridorm," a building with the boys on one side, the girls on the other, and a cafeteria and an old battle-axe of a house mother determinedly in between.

Denver is a private university originally founded as a Methodist church school. Tuition was about $750 a quarter when I was going there. Pretty rich. And without a full athletic scholarship, I couldn't ever have afforded it. But, fortunately, hockey is their big spectator sport, though the ski team, under Coach Willie Schaeffler, has won something like 11 or 12 national championships over the last 15 years. Still, hockey draws the paying crowds. And the whole time I was at Denver, 5205 rabid fans packed the Arena for every one of our 20 home games each season, a monied group of supporters with a great many Denver graduates among them. On its own scale, Denver is a great hockey town. Of course, hockey is what covers most of the athletic department's bills; and, not surprisingly, the players are practically all Canadians.

I have to chuckle when I hear talk about Canadian "ringers" playing for American colleges. Even the Harvard hockey playing hero in "Love Story," Oliver Barret, takes a swipe at "all those Canadian whores" up at Cornell. Some love story! But it cuts another way, too. What if we'd left you to play your rinky-dink version of our game in the colleges down here? Why, even now, "foreigners" like me are regarded as traitors in my own country for taking the soft way out.

Consequently, one of my greatest satisfactions at Denver came when I was hockey captain my senior year: We beat the Canadian National team 4–1. The team was absolutely loaded with the pick of Canada's best junior players. That night we helped change the image of American college hockey.

People may ask, as indeed they do, if it is really American hockey out there. Well, it's certainly being played in America. Technically, though, just about the only true-born Americans playing in the powerful Western College Hockey Association are Minnesota boys. Everyone else is Canadian. But look at the East, where teams like Cornell that were hardly a scrimmage only a few years ago are contenders today; and, yes, just loaded with "Canadian whores."

All this puzzles me, however. Would you rather pay to see the L.A. Rams or the Middletown Pipers play football? It's a simple fact of business that isn't lost on college athletic departments or fans buying the tickets. People want to see the best brand of hockey available. I don't think they worry too much whether the players are from Europe, Slobovia, America or Canada. The fact is that Canadians still supply the best game of hockey, and Americans are demanding it today as never before.

Perhaps if the present hockey boom continues in this country, American youngsters will soon become NHL material. But at present the motivation, the hunger, the same kind of profound national hockey tradition that a young Canadian discovers at birth, simply doesn't exist in the country.

I remember our freshman games against Colorado, a team of Americans who had simply not grown up in the rough, tough Canadian tradition. We soon let them know we were on the ice by running at them every chance we got. And if an American came out for the Denver team, we'd give him a hard time, too. Nothing dirty, mind you, just good hard checks. And if he couldn't hack the hitting, he'd leave. Quite a few did.

Murray, however, didn't care where a man came from. He chose his players for their attitude: believing as he did, that a person with desire can learn much faster and eventually outperform a player with greater talent but a poor approach.

Of course, Murray Armstrong was an excellent coach. He'd played in the NHL back in the '40s and early '50s. And his assistant, Harry Ottenbriet, had also fooled around the minors a bit before coming to Denver as a student, although he didn't play college hockey because somebody in Montreal squealed on him and he was declared ineligible for NCAA competition. But he pushed his way on through law school just the same.

Harry had a profound influence on preparing me for the pros. And today he's the business manager as well as legal adviser for both Cliff and myself.

But Denver hockey was mostly Murray. There were never such hockey practices as his. I remember one particular conditioning torture called "the hops," a complicated race between different waves of players, which concluded with an end-to-end sprint. A real man-killer.

The Denver varsity had a mediocre season my freshman year. We weren't part of the team, but we'd practice with them and occasionally play against them. We actually *beat* them several times during the season; people said we were the best freshman team in Denver history.

This didn't help the varsity much, however. There

were seniors that year who had played Juniors in Canada before even coming to college. They were in their middle 20's, a pretty hard-nosed, fast bunch whose habits opened my eyes pretty fast.

Cliff remembers only too well. He was a 19-year-old sophomore at the time, his first year on the team. During practices, when Murray would be giving instructions down at the other end of the rink, these older guys would be slouching around muttering obscenities.

It made me furious to hear all this because I'd been brought up to respect my elders. And on the ice, you do what the coach says. He's got that right over you. And if he's no good, it will out. I've always liked the expression "Time wounds all heels." Lousy coaches are no exceptions.

Players just hurt themselves when they carve up a team with bad feelings. From the beginning, I found Murray a superior person. So when I heard all this back-stabbing going on, I made up my mind right then: "I'm going to work hard for you, Murray Armstrong, and next year we're going to be a winner." I said it only to myself, of course. But when I make up my mind, I'm a very stubborn guy.

Before I begin sounding too noble, however, perhaps I'd better mention a few of the bonehead things I did to earn me "The Riddler" tag. Some, in fact, prompted a few people to suggest that maybe I was mentally retarded.

None Against!

I guess one of the most famous early incidents happened my freshman year. After Christmas break, Dad had let me drive an old car back from Saskatoon to use around campus. A month or so later I was out with the Baptist Church group for a bowling night. The alley was on a hill above a busy intersection, and though I parked the car in gear, I neglected to use the emergency brake.

We all had a good time for a couple of hours—I rolled a couple of 100 games—but when I came out, the car wasn't there. Stolen! I'd never had anything stolen before in my life. The church people were all very kind, and called the police to report the missing car.

The cops came right over and I sat in their cruiser, showing them my Saskatchewan driver's permit, the license plate numbers, everything. Then the cop did a little chewing on me because I apparently should have reregistered my car in the States by this time. So the atmosphere is a little strained.

Suddenly this man comes running up yelling, "There's a car in my house!" Over and over again, "There's a car in my house!"

"What kind of plates does it have?" asks the cop.

"Suskunia . . . Saskachewny . . ." the guy can't pronounce it, although he has it written down on a scrap of paper, license number and all.

"Saskatchewan?" the cop asks.

"Yeah! That's it!" says the guy. And he starts reading

off the plate number. I can't believe it. Then he describes how he'd been sitting watching television and this car comes rolling right into his living room. No driver.

Well, by this time I was just shaking. Of course I had an insurance policy on the car, but $200 deductible. Here I was working in sorority kitchens for meals and picking up about $20 a month. Just barely scraping by. A movie was a big evening for me. No dinner. I always had that in the sorority kitchen. As well as lunch, if I wanted to wash dishes afterwards. But, anyway, my car had apparently slipped a gear and just started traveling down the hill. The incredible thing was that it had missed everything while coasting across the intersection. Then it had hit another slope, and at the bottom was this guy's house. The car must have gathered quite a head of steam by this time. I could picture the guy relaxing in his chair; and then just imagine the explosion of the car breaking and entering.

The cop takes these stolen car forms and rips them in half right in front of my nose. "Well, I guess that takes care of this case," he says rather sarcastically. But he was pretty nice: No charges were pressed against me. And the guy himself turned out to be a big Denver hockey fan who actually helped me find a tow truck to pull the car out of his house. In fact, he even admitted later that he was delighted about the whole thing. Apparently, the busted part of the house had needed fixing for some time, only he couldn't afford it. This way, he got one new wall for nothing.

I didn't dare tell Pop about it for almost two months. People get weak hearts as they grow older, I told myself. And I could remember all the times I'd seen him mad: His face would get so red I was sure he was going to have a heart attack. So there were a lot of things I'd try to spare him from for as long as possible. And then, when I finally just had to get it off my conscience, I'd often tell Mom first.

In this case I wrote to the insurance company myself. Believe me, it was a hard letter to write. How to explain what I'd done? Well, this time Dad found out about it before I told him. One day his insurance man called him up and happened to mention, "By the way, Joe, the car's almost fixed." I'm glad I wasn't home at the time.

Sophomore year saw some radical changes in my life. I really tumbled from Grace, straight down like in my dreams. You might almost say I became reckless.

The five of us Saskatooners still lived together, but now we were in that corridorm with the gate-keeping housemother. Actually she proved only a modest obstacle, because we'd all devised any number of ways to signal each other out of windows.

By now Dawn and I were seeing each other regularly. Up to this point I'd never really had a girl friend. My dates just didn't seem to want to stay around for very long. Maybe it was the fact that hockey would always be my first love—and no girl likes to stand second to anybody or anything. Dawn is the first one I ever knew who really didn't mind.

In order to be alone, we'd sometimes visit the training room at the rink, for which I had a set of keys. Towels, bandages, linaments and rest tables were everywhere. Not exactly the ideal setting for romance. But we were happy just to be together, and this became one of our favorite places.

And there were other good times, rare escapes together off on "woodsies" as we called them, trips to the Rockies in the spring. Maybe Vail or Winter Park or Aspen, which were fun in the late cornsnow season. Dawn would help with expenses. She was very generous in her understanding of my situation.

We skied, of course. How can you live in Colorado and not? She was very good. I kept after it. I ski the way I skate: wide and fast. No form at all but what incredible fun. During the long hockey season, my face gets as tough as hide. I like to think it's windburn from the slopes.

I remember one woodsie when my teammate Craig Patrick and his girl, together with Dawn and I, spent the weekend at this cabin belonging to Chuck Lamson, who was playing for the L.A. Rams at the time. We didn't do any skiing because it was still in the heart of hockey season. But we had snowball fights under the tall, spreading pine trees around the cabin, and built a huge snowman with charcoal eyes and a big cigar for a nose. Just a little break in the hockey season. Two days. But two days I don't believe any of us will ever forget.

The bad times were usually my doing. One of the team jokes had to do with how our relationship was always breaking up.

I'm sorry about all this now. Dawn was good for me. She worked with me when I had trouble in certain courses, and would type my reports for these classes. And all the time she kept coming back. She did everything. If I gave anything of myself, she'd return it tenfold. That's how she was. She's the only girl I've ever truly loved.

But now back to "The Riddler," who was beginning to do a little beer drinking. And like a lot of first-timers I went completely overboard, especially when it came to chug-a-lug contests. One guy in particular, Don Cameron, enjoyed taking me on. I have a fierce competitive attitude about even such recreational diversions as Ping-Pong, so you know what a sitting duck I was.

We'd sit across a table, full beer glasses in front of us, until someone would say "Go!" And every time, before I was more than a couple of swallows down, I'd hear Cameron's empty glass slamming on the table. Unbelievable! I even looked up the world record and found that some 31-year-old Englishman back in 1957 had downed 2¼ pints of ale in 10 seconds flat. Cameron must have been even faster. "Let's try it again," he'd say calmly. The same thing would happen.

I refused to give up, of course, until I could barely hear the "let's try again." Quite a few contests later I finally discovered his secret. All this time he'd been sitting there holding an empty glass under the table. "The switch" is one of the oldest tricks in the world. I didn't know it.

The Canadian hockey players tended to stick close together. We represented a sort of informal fraternity and our parties were popular. Girls found us unpredictable and more fun. We seemed less programmed than our American classmates and were able to let go and just be ourselves. In short, we were pretty loose.

One of our favorite hangouts was the Stadium Inn, with its sawdust floor and quarter-a-game pool table. And Leo's Barber Shop, where Leo Bayer would counsel us on all sorts of problems, lend us a few bucks for a date or a weekend, and do everything he could to keep his hockey players out of trouble and in school.

Leo's was two blocks from campus, and during class breaks we'd stroll over and sit around reading magazines or jawing away. It was our social center, our small-town pot-bellied stove. I'll never forget the year I graduated. I'd started karate training as part of my preparation for the pros, and, naturally, Leo wanted to see how good I was.

He always kept a few hockey sticks in the back of his shop. So he took one and propped it between two chairs and said, "Okay, let's see your chop." Nothing to it, I thought. I'd already broken quite a few boards in class. The trick, of course, is to hit along the grain—to work up your concentration and energy and . . . *"aay-yeee!" Thunk!* . . . come down hard on the natural split of the wood.

But hockey sticks are made to survive a certain amount of abuse, a fact I didn't consider at the time. So here were all these players clustered around to witness the main event. I stood over the stick, breathing hard, getting all psyched up for my yell. Well, when the edge of my hand came down, it bounced right back up. Damaged pride, damaged hand and hoots of laughter.

The Ninth Hole was another favorite hangout. An informal drinking spot with a decidedly masculine atmosphere and lots of pictures of Denver hockey players (to which large blowups of Cliff and me have now been added wearing our Black Hawk uniforms). The owner, Al Mares, was a real booster.

I remember one Sunday afternoon in the spring after we'd all been playing a little baseball. Sitting around the Hole, we began wondering exactly how far it was back to the campus. Someone guessed about three miles. "I bet I can run it in 20 minutes," I said.

I'd never been much of a runner. However, one of my private heroes had always been the great Australian distance runner Herb Elliot, who used to train something like 26 miles a day through swamps and deep sand and up mountains. Of course, I'd stopped racing years before this, when I became too slow to challenge anyone.

But here were all these guys willing to bet me a pitcher of beer each that I couldn't make the time. So at the signal I set off running barefoot across grass, gravel and hot pavement. One of the players had given me his key; and I was to phone them when I arrived. I placed the call with a minute and a half to spare. Not bad. Three six-minute miles and I've forgotten how many pitchers of beer.

Next day in a class on athletic injuries, the topic happened to be how to treat blisters. By coincidence, I had at least seven on each foot and could barely walk when I arrived. That I should become the class guinea pig was immediately approved with but one dissenting vote.

It took four of the biggest guys to hold me down while each blister was slit open and iodine poured under the skin. When I began yelling, Gene Bradshaw, the instructor, jammed a towel in my mouth. Actually, however, I'd say the demonstration was more a faith healing than anything else. From scarcely being able to walk, I literally ran away from that table. Bradshaw does it again!

None of us will ever forget Gene Bradshaw, our

trainer. He was about 50 years old, carried a big gut, stood 5' 8" and weighed close to 230 pounds. Strong as an ox, and an ex-paratrooper, he had a Yul Brynner shave and kept a bottle in his cabinet. He called it the "nectar of the gods." We called it Old Fitzgerald.

When you got a rub from Gene, you really knew it. He swore by tough skin and all sorts of hot linaments. And when he began to rub, he'd begin to boil—until he had to pause for a drop of nectar. After which he'd go *"phhiifff . . ."* and come back rubbing harder than ever.

No one ever talked back to this Sumo wrestler. And when anyone got out of line, he'd suddenly grab them to his belly and knock their wind out. He also kept this sawed-off hockey stick around to club us on those occasions when he thought we needed it.

My first year, I got the stick a lot. Freshmen were *never* supposed to bother the trainer. But you know me. I'd be in there asking a lot of questions when, suddenly, *whap!* Another time I stupidly disobeyed his standing orders and went out to practice without full equipment. Ass. Sure enough, I got blasted by a shot in the ankle. It began to swell quite badly and Gene wasn't around. So I asked one of the varsity what to do.

"Put your shoes on, Maggy, and run home on it," he said. "That's the best way to get over it." Of course, when I got home my ankle was the size of a balloon. Gene was furious. I'd been an ass once again, and really got the stick this time.

Murray, Denver and Dawn

Everyone liked Gene tremendously. He was really a very gentle person who'd been through a lot, but now loved his life. There was a time during my junior year when the team bus got stranded in the middle of a blizzard near Duluth, Minnesota. Gene was right across the aisle from me, sitting back remarkably relaxed, or so it seemed. He gave me this mischievous little wink. "Nectar of the gods," he murmured.

I developed a fascination for gambling at college, something I'd never done at home. Poker, gin rummy, dogs and horses—you name it. But no beginner's luck, I'm afraid. Early on, I lost $100. It was the dogs that cost me. So all spring quarter I went out caddying—sometimes 36 holes a day with a bag on each shoulder.

Still, I'd take a bet on just about anything except our own hockey games. For example, several friends thought I had the largest appetite they'd ever seen. Undoubtedly this capacity had a lot to do with Murray's incredible workouts. But it's true that eating was one of my favorite occupations, which fortunately was also part of the hashing-job deal. Anyway, at a party one night, Jimmy Wiste starts promoting my appetite. He does such a good job in fact that suddenly everyone wants to bet I can't eat 30 hard-boiled eggs in 30 minutes. Done! Someone gets the eggs. Jimmy holds the money. The timer gives the signal.

Jimmy and I have worked all this out beforehand, of course. "You really think you can do it, Maggy?" Sure.

With five minutes to go and five eggs left I start to choke a little. Jimmy offers to raise the bets and everyone agrees. I then finish the last five eggs inside of two minutes. Jimmy and I split the winnings fifty-fifty.

Well, back to Murray, who in a number of ways is not unlike Billy Reay—though Murray is dealing with impressionable college boys, while Billy is obliged to treat his players like the men they're supposed to be. Both, however, prefer to sit back and study things a bit before taking action. Like the old saying: The first mistake is "shame on me," after that it's "shame on you." I think this is the best attitude a coach can have. You wrong me once, okay. Twice you're in trouble.

Another thing. Neither has to say very much. They've both got these penetrating eyes that pierce you to the core; any player who cares can read one of those glances. A compliment for something you've done makes the day, and you really work for such moments under these fellows. Otherwise, not much can really be explained; a properly motivated hockey player should know inside himself whether he's playing well or not.

Of the two, Murray is the more impassioned speaker, sort of a Knute Rockne style—which is, after all, better suited to college than the pros. Murray would always list specific objectives for each game and then tell us in no uncertain terms to think of absolutely *nothing else* all the day before. "Work as hard as you can out there," he'd say. "Give 100 percent . . . and when it's over, win or lose, if you can look straight in a mirror and tell yourself you've given all you had, then you're a winner. . . ."

I'm sure all coaches try to get this across, but Murray had a special talent for it. There'd always be considerable emotion in his voice—never too loud, never uncontrolled, but inspired. And he'd really work himself up for these speeches, not just to the team but to other groups as well. He was a compelling, forceful speaker.

Billy does this too. And when either makes a general comment, you somehow feel it's being directed at you personally. Naturally, if anything needs to be said to a player, it's done privately in a way best suited to the individual's personality. A private affair between player and coach from which a special brand of mutual respect and confidence will then start to build.

Murray always got my 100 percent. But midway through sophomore year, I discovered that he'd been watching me a good deal more closely than I had realized. And, finally, he came right out with the fact that he was frankly rather disappointed in my performance. This came right after a weekend series of back-to-back games against one of our chief rivals, Michigan Tech. Both games were played on their tiny rink in Houghton, the heart of copper country; and their great All-American, Tony Esposito, was in goal for them. So you can bet they had a powerhouse.

Now Denver had a large rink, well suited to our wide-open style of play. Tech's, on the other hand, was so small that you had to make your plays fast or they'd be smothered. And between periods the fans would all lock arms and sing this Copper Country Ballad of theirs, swaying back and forth as they did so. You could swear the whole stadium was going to come tumbling down. Pretty awesome seeing it for the first time.

Anyhow, most of us had a bit too much to drink celebrating our pair of victories. Especially me. And the next morning, when I tried to toss my equipment bag on the bus, I spun along right after it. Murray was missing none of this. Naturally, too, the whole team was placing bets on who'd be the first one to throw up. No contest. I did before our little prop charter even left the ground. And I was in the seat right next to Murray when it happened.

We took the prop to Minneapolis, then changed to a big jet for Denver. This time Murray had fixed it so I *had* to sit next to him. "You know, if you play it right," he began saying quietly as we rose from the ground, "you can have quite a future in hockey. You've got all the credentials: desire, determination, you want to learn and don't mind working hard. But just look at yourself right now." I was embarrassed to the point of mortification.

A couple of things he stressed particularly. "I'm disappointed in your academic performance this year," he went on in that same even tone of his. He knew all about it. My grades were indeed down. I wasn't used to America's three quarters system, where you had to study hard each part of the year in order to do well. I felt I was just getting into a subject when suddenly it would all be over. There was no more cramming at the end of the year to pass, like in my last high school year. Murray and I discussed these things.

"And you've got to start taking better care of yourself," he said. "I don't mind my players enjoying themselves, letting off steam and having a few beers once in a while, but you're running around half-cocked. And the point is," he added, "there's a great *pro future* waiting for you, if you'll but work for it."

Maybe he said some other things, too, but I don't remember listening. "Pro future" kept ringing in my head. Talk of those proverbial stars in one's eyes, they were certainly in mine then—because of what Murray Armstrong had said to me.

Murray gives advice without necessarily expecting you'll take it. But if you do, you're likely to be given increased responsibility. In this case, I took his advice quite seriously and began to moderate my habits and improve my scholastic record. From then on he spoke to me more often, and a close relationship began developing between us. On the day of home games, for instance, the team always had a steak together in the early afternoon at a Denver hotel called Writers Manor. Afterwards most of the players would jalopie back to campus.

None Against!

Murray drove a very distinctive old Cadillac, which he refused to turn in for a newer model. He always felt that if anyone ever hit him he wouldn't get hurt even if the other guy was killed. Often he'd ask me to join him on the trip home, and then he'd question me about how things were going, or tell me how very much he wanted to win a particular game. I began to see that he really believed in me, and I tried to relay the message on the ice by playing the best hockey I knew.

I in turn asked him any number of personal things: whether he thought I should marry Dawn, should I buy an old car. He'd offer his advice, and I'd pretty near always follow it.

Murray also slipped me a few extra responsibilities on the side. One I was particularly glad to have, because it paid quite a bit of money. Old Timer's Night.

Sunday nights a group of Denver businessmen would come out to play. Murray asked me to advise them, referee their games and suggest light workouts. At $20 a night! A small fortune. Sometimes Murray would show up too, and we'd all just fool around. It was a lot of fun.

One night I tossed my weighted puck on the ice while the Old Timers were practicing. They started shooting and passing it around like an ordinary item. Well, a couple of guys took slapshots, and their sticks just shattered. "Just not making sticks the way they used to," they muttered. "Stinking wood!" I never did tell them about the puck. Of course Murray knew, but we kept it between us.

We didn't win the NCAAs my sophomore year. We had a good season, but lost to North Dakota in the play-offs. Murray thought we had the better team but that too many guys were already thinking ahead to the spring break in Mazatlán, Mexico. Probably he was right.

For a number of years, in fact, quite a few Denver players had been spending their spring holidays in Mazatlán, and I joined the tradition. It was quite an experience for me, seeing what part of Mexico was like and getting my first real taste of independent travel.

A caravan of us drove down to the Arizona border town of Nogales, then boarded one of those smoky old Mexican trains for the remainder of the trip. It was an unforgettable, lurching 24-hour journey south across Sonora Province and on down through desert-dry Culia-cán in the Sinaloa District to Mazatlán on the Pacific Coast. The best way to see a country and its people is to take a slow train like this one, tequila and all.

Mazatlán was great. Beach-living among the sun gods, playing volley ball with the hordes of surfers who pour down every spring with their boards and girls. The place is a surfing Mecca. Everything from Muscle Beach to Cheese Cake.

But for me there were some unpleasant aspects as well. I had a perpetual battle with diarrhea and was sunburned to a crisp, my fair complexion peeling like a snake, and I was shivering with fever. I even had a few doubts I was going to survive. Still, it was a lot of fun, and there's no question but that I matured a bit during the course of it all.

My last two college years I lived off-campus, first with Cliff and Jimmy Wiste and a guy named Dave Rosenthal, who all graduated a year ahead of me, then with hockey players Craig Patrick, Jerry Powers, Jeff Jennings and Cab Stitt. We were to win the NCAAs both years.

Murray began holding his "lemon and orange" contests about this time. They'd always come the day before a game and right at the end of practice. He'd have us all line up for breakaways on the goalie. Whoever scored would go to the "oranges" side of the rink. Those who didn't would join the "lemons" on the other side. Then it was simply a matter of elimination: the orange award went to the guy who scored the most breakaway goals. Murray would next challenge the lemons until only one man was left, the lemon who hadn't scored at all.

Another institution was the Game Puck Award. It was presented to the player who, in the opinion of his teammates, had committed the outstandingly dumb move of the game. My goaltender roommate, Jerry Powers, received it for letting a few easy ones slip past him. Another time I got it after I broke my stick and then proceeded to carry it around for half a shift without even realizing it. Pretty unconscious, Maggy. One of the funniest, however, was Craig Patrick's Puck Award. While going over the boards, he'd heard Murray yell to stop. He stopped all right, landing headfirst on the ice as he tried to scramble back to the bench. An hilarious performance. The vote was unanimous that time.

My first exposure to international hockey came when we played in a Colorado Springs exhibition tournament against the Swedish, Finnish, American and Russian national teams over the Christmas holidays in my junior year. We beat everyone until we lost to Russia in the finals. Facing them was an unforgettable experience. Their approach to hockey consists of pinpoint passing between strong, muscular skaters who just never seem to get tired. Denver played a good game, but the Russians scored two quick power-play goals. International rules prohibit a short-handed team from icing the puck without being called for it. And they then went on to outclass us 8–2.

If I were to rate the best hockey teams in the world today, I'd have to put the Russians right up beside Boston, New York, Chicago and Montreal.

I'll never forget watching them prepare for that game against us in Colorado Springs. The morning of the game itself, they were out running around the lake. Then they did about an hour of calisthenics before even lacing on their skates for an additional ice workout. The day of the game, mind you.

Their team officials kept a very close guard on them. The players seemed to want to talk to us, but they weren't allowed to. Could the officials have been afraid that we might try to sell their players on the bright future for hockey in America? Obviously the Party boss wouldn't want his young stars to know much about this aspect of the capitalistic system, because just about any of the Russians could make the NHL—and a few could become real stars.

About the only strike against the Russian players was all the Coke they drank with their steaks at the training table. I've simply got to find some way to convert them to the Un-cola drink when next we meet. But kidding aside, playing these fellows did wonders for us. They demonstrated a whole new way to play the game. We hadn't really known what condition meant. And they'd refined puck control to an art. There were things to learn and boundaries to extend. The net result was that Denver completed its season without losing a single game—29 straight wins, an all-time NCAA record.

My Denver years were so much fun that it's tempting to ramble on and make this book a sequel to "Tom Brown's School Days" or "Dink Stover at Yale." Well, I'm not through yet, because there are a few more recollections that stand out above the others. One of which, I guess, has to be the single greatest moment in my life.

Murray, Denver and Dawn

This was in Duluth right after the NCAA playoffs, the year Cliff and Jimmy Wiste were co-captains. After two scoreless periods Denver broke the game wide open, to best the North Dakota Sioux 4–0. None Against! The first time I've ever cried as an adult. In fact, everyone was crying and hugging each other, including Murray. All season long he'd been psyching us up for this moment, saying we'd never forget it as long as we lived. He was right.

It was the same kind of incredible team effort that the Black Hawks were able to muster to win the Prince of Wales trophy my rookie year. I cried that time too. And I'll never forget when Stan Mikita entered the dressing room afterwards and said, "I think we should all thank God for our success and happiness at this moment." We all prayed, bowing our heads in silence. For a moment you could have heard a pin drop.

Back in Duluth, however, none of us were yet pros. No money in it, just college kids doing it on pride. And what a team it was—with 10 of us playing in the pros today. There were more NHL scouts at the finals than at any previous college game in history.

We won the NCAAs again my senior year when I was captain. This time in the finals we beat Cornell, who had All-American Ken Dryden in the nets. There were even more scouts in the stands at Colorado Springs than the previous year. Chicago's Tommy Ivan was one of them. It was not that we had a better team, mind you, but college hockey was now recognized to be an important farm system in its own right. Players could now come from the classroom directly to the NHL. I might add, believe it or not, that I scored more points in those playoffs than any forward and received the MVP Award.

But it was actually an earlier game against North Dakota that provided the most inspiring moment for me personally. The Sioux had to be just about our toughest regular season opponent, and this time we were playing them at Grand Forks, an unbelievably cold rink. You'd be frozen when you came into the dressing room between periods. Most of us wore earmuffs or woolen hats under our helmets. Their rink was in pretty sad shape. I remember one visit when they'd just finished painting their box seat section a bright pea green, and Murray commented that it was like putting earrings on a pig.

With us on this trip was centerman Bob Trembecky, one of our best forwards who had been ineligible to play because of poor grades the previous quarter. By now, however, and with some special academic help, he'd made a recovery. So any moment we were expecting a call from University Chancellor Mitchell, giving Trembecky the go-ahead to play. Mr. Mitchell, not so incidentally, was one of the team's strongest supporters; consequently we weren't anticipating any problem.

But someone screwed up, and the chancellor wasn't contacted. So the call never came. I drove to the rink with Murray. Timmy Gould was along as well as a friend of Murray's. It was dark and quiet in the car. Suddenly I felt Murray's hand squeeze my shoulder. A shudder ran down my spine. Murray was asking me for a special kind of help. Not a word passed between us, yet I've never experienced such a feeling of trust in all my life. Talk about being psyched up! That night, without Trembecky, we won 2–0, and I assisted on both goals.

Murray had a dry sense of humor that kept us right on our toes. Perhaps the best example of this came after our exhibition game against the Czechs my senior year. The Czechs are one strong team—they even beat the Russians in a cliff-hanger. The score is tied 2–2 in the third period. Suddenly there's a misunderstanding over a penalty against them. A Czech had come out of the box before serving his full time, and the referee is trying to explain this to their coach through an interpreter. All at once the Czechs abruptly skated off the ice.

We stayed on the ice fooling around for about 30 minutes until Murray finally decided, "Okay. That's it. We've given them enough time. They forfeit the game." He was right, of course, and officially, we were awarded the contest 3–2.

But just as soon as we'd left the ice, out came the Czechs again. We're all undressed, ready for the showers, when in walks the President of U.S. Amateur Hockey.

"Murray! Murray! You better get everybody back out there. The Czechs want to play."

Murray simply gestured toward his assistant, Harry Ottenbriet, who was barely out of law school and rather overcome by all this. "Don't talk to me, sir," Murray said quietly. "Take the matter up with my lawyer here."

I managed to stash quite a few honors at Denver: Sophomore of the Year in college hockey, regional All-Star for three years and All-American twice. *The Clarion,* Denver's college newspaper, voted me Senior of the Year, Hockey Player of the Year and Athlete of the Year. These among others. I was a pretty fortunate guy.

But one must always remember that the glorious moments in a person's life are not so many. The game keeps moving on. And as I've said before, you're only as good as your last shift even in the best of times. And there will always be the disappointments as well.

Ironically, one of the unhappiest moments for me came right in the middle of all this college excitement. My parents had driven down to see us play at Colorado Springs in that international tournament. They were involved in an accident: Dad had a black eye and Mom a bad back.

Dawn was to meet them for the first time. I was so sure everything would go well and, at first anyway, they seemed to be getting along fine. But one evening, after I'd left them alone together, they began talking about religion. Dawn did not practice a formal faith.

And suddenly they turned against her. She wasn't a Christian, they said.

That Christmas was one of the saddest days of my life.

CHAPTER 5

Harry and Me

Harry Ottenbriet has had a most important, though very specialized, influence on me: It was Harry who hand-tailored my present policeman's image and masterminded me into the pros. This began with an intensive training program toward the end of my senior year; included several rough negotiation sessions with Tommy Ivan, one of the shrewdest general managers of them all; and came to an end that same autumn when I signed my first Black Hawk contract.

I followed Harry's instructions like a robot. And these fast few months proved a remarkable period of intrigue and strategy by anyone's standards—even Agatha Christie's. Harry was to coin the "Red Raider" sobriquet, which would become the turning point toward all the good things that life has granted me today.

Harry, of course, was Murray's assistant my four

years at Denver. He knew exactly how long and how hard we should practice at any one time, and he never dwelt on elements that were not absolutely essential to a sound college game. He'd make certain that a specific fundamental was well implanted before moving on to something else. If this took two weeks, it took two weeks. But when he was done, you had it down pat.

Probably the most valuable lesson Harry taught me was how to hip-check properly. This certainly was a help in college, but you seldom catch players with their heads down in the pros. At Denver, however, this became one of my specialities.

Harry also taught me the trick of starting to run at a man who was crossing the blue-line with the puck. "Wave your stick to distract him and to keep him from going straight," he'd tell me. "He'll instinctively shy away from the stick and head right for your body if you do it right. Then aim for his chest with your shoulder and, at the last instant, turn your hip sideways right across his thighs." I built my college reputation around this maneuver and could really plaster guys, sometimes even sending them off for repairs.

So I took to Harry, who, like Murray, was always direct and did his best to keep me threading the straight and narrow. Another thing too: having played the minors, he was no babe with regard to the senior leagues. He knew only too well, for example, that college hockey is wide-open. A defenseman can simply carry the puck over his own blue-line or shoot it all the way up ice to a forward and catch the opposition sleeping—like a quarterback throwing the bomb.

Pro play is quite different. Offside and icing rules are vastly more strict. The game is much more positional, but at the same time a defenseman can be knocked silly by an offensive check in his own zone—something the American college game does not allow. "But it's no extraordinary adjustment," Harry would say, "if you can learn to carry the puck with your *head up*." True. And thanks again, Harry.

The year I graduated, Harry was fresh out of Denver Law School. One day late in that last season, he showed me a magazine article on Bobby Orr's agent-lawyer, Al Eagleson, who is now head of the NHL Players' Association. The idea of agents for hockey players was a very new thing at this time, of course. So we talked for a while about how hockey players were easily the most underpaid athletes in professional sport, and Harry said something simple like, "We'll make them pay, Maggy."

Right then, you might say, our partnership was formed: a certain yearly percentage to him for handling my interests, and a willingness on my part to follow his instructions to the letter. We sealed it with a handshake, the only formal business gesture that has ever passed between us. The best single decision of my life. And Cliff was to join Harry the following year.

Unlike so many representatives, Harry truly believes that personal friendship and absolute trust are part and parcel of any sound business relationship. He'd never want to do this kind of thing full-time or start one of these impersonal agencies that handle a whole stable of players: "Okay, here's contract number 34. Let's get it over with." Harry says, "Okay, here's Keith's contract. Now let's see what might best suit him." I've never questioned his judgment or motives in all the time we've been together. He admits to being a bit of a frustrated player today, and once told me: "What you are doing is part of me because it's something I could never do myself."

Our strategy began just before the 1969 NCAA finals, which we took from Cornell at Colorado Springs. Harry knew Tommy Ivan would be in the stands, and he told me that if he approached me afterwards I should suggest we meet the following day back in Denver when my lawyer would be present.

Sure enough, right after the game, here's Tommy in the dressing room. I followed Harry's instructions and Tommy seemed rather surprised. Nevertheless, we settled on joining at the Denver Hilton where he was staying. Tommy must have known this would be my first real exposure to a professional proposition. What he probably didn't know, however, was that it would be Harry's baptism as well. We were both rookies in the rawest sense of the word.

None Against!

But Harry, who'd worked his way through law school as a claims adjuster for an insurance company, wasn't as uneasy as I. He knew a few of the subtleties about the negotiation process. And he also has an uncanny natural ability to read what people are thinking. After one session he knows exactly what someone is like and just how to manipulate the proceedings. Besides all his years in the minors, he's also been his own representative during contract conferences. In short, he was coming into this first meeting pretty well equipped.

We drove back to Denver together the next morning and Harry began to show me exactly how much homework he'd been up to. He laid all the facts before me. Here it was, still March, and with my own last amateur season just ended. Undoubtedly Chicago would invite me to come in for one of those five-game tryouts. But look at the team right now, he counseled. For players of that caliber to be last in the league was shocking. And equally inexplicable was the team's 246 goals-against record. Compare that figure to the two-year old expansion clubs: Pittsburgh—252; Minnesota—270; California—251; Los Angeles—260. And look at Philadelphia's 225 and the St. Louis Blue's 157, with Chicago's former great Glenn Hall in their goal. Obviously, the Black Hawks overall defensive setup was a mess. Of course, Pit Martin hadn't made his revealing statements yet, about favoritism on the team. So Chicago's plight was still an enormous mystery to such outsiders as Harry and me.

But candid as ever, Harry also said that I simply wasn't ready yet. He didn't think I could fight worth a darn. I was strong, but I wasn't tough. I wasn't mentally prepared for the professional ordeal. Certain old pros would just love to crucify a brash young rookie—especially one right out of college who is not used to being hit in his own end, yet at the same time is being heralded as a potential shot-in-the-arm. Certainly someone would test me, explained Harry, and I'd probably get creamed, thereby ruining that all-important first impression that can last forever. Sometimes they simply won't try you again, no matter what you do. So there was no way Harry would let me go to Chicago right then. And the rest of his plans I was not to discover until we were actually face to face with Tommy in his room at the Hilton.

That afternoon was almost as nerve-wracking as a Stanley Cup final game. My heart was right up there in my throat the whole time. Of course, I never stopped to think that Tommy was taking special pains to meet with Harry and me in the first place. Now I can laugh because I know Tommy pretty well. He has a job to do and he must seem very hard about it. He's dealing out money, so he just can't afford to be as close to the players as Billy Reay.

Management usually thinks less of us than we do ourselves. Hockey players often have dreams of grandeur, and it's Tommy's job to prick these illusions. Players may get under-dealt in the process, just as sometimes they get too much—though not that often when Tommy's in charge. Still, my dealings with him have always resulted in fairness. Furthermore, his word is his bond.

But there's one part of this business every player wants to avoid. It's that final phase of a hopelessly dead-locked salary dispute called arbitration, when the matter is turned over to a league-appointed attorney. Harry and I approached this just once, before the start of my third season.

Now stop and think about it. Here's a lawyer hired by the league coming in to arbitrate. Who pays his salary? Management. So who's going to benefit? You guessed it. Consequently, you want to settle matters on your own if you possibly can. On this particular occasion I wound up with a realistic two-year agreement somewhere between our original positions.

Needless to say, Harry was our spokesman that first meeting. Tommy would try to intimidate us, he warned. How true. Tommy, in fact, opened the discussion by saying that my chances of playing with the Hawks at that time were almost nil, but Chicago would like to take a look at me anyway for possible future use. He made the hope seem faint indeed.

Tommy's manner was as hard-nosed as his voice. Sort of the Jimmy Cagney routine, only Tommy was too well dressed. Nothing gaudy, mind you; just prim and proper and pin-striped. His hair was slicked back. In fact his total appearance was outstanding.

Harry and Me

Tommy Ivan sat there saying little: formidable, hard to read, and very intimidating to a novice like me. He had it all together. Those dark beady eyes of his that have been sizing up the professional hockey world for more than 30 years were darting between Harry and me like a hawk lining up two prairie chickens. Distinctly noncommital. Without Harry, I'd have given up right there and taken whatever Tommy was offering.

Sure enough, up comes the subject of the five-game tryout. And I can't believe what Harry does. He tells Tommy that the tryout suggestion is fine provided Magnuson gets paid $1000 per game and signs a two-year, $80,000 contract the following day. The figure is patently exorbitant. But in the brief silence that follows, I began seeing money signs. I was in debt at the time, had a few loans outstanding, and could not even conceive of the kind of money Harry was throwing around so lightly.

Tommy jumps out of his chair. "It appears, Magnuson, that you don't want to play for the Chicago Black Hawks." This he says looking directly at me as if Harry wasn't even in the room. "Oh no! . . . I mean, yes . . . ," I exclaimed, somewhat flustered. I even manage to explain that my skates and bag are down in Harry's car and that I'm ready to take whatever flight back to Chicago he's going to be on.

"Right," Harry interrupts, cutting me off. "As long as we can agree on those amounts." Of course, we never could. The fact is, Tommy never offered anything at all. He just left it that maybe he would be seeing us again at training camp in the fall, which is exactly the way Harry wanted it.

Leaving the Hilton, however, I was somewhat upset. Those money signs that had seemed so close had disappeared awfully fast. For just a moment there, I'd felt it floating in my hands. Harry explained that they *never* offer you anything. They want to see you first. Even then you can have the most spectacular tryout in history and be offered peanuts. They'll make excuses like: "Oh, well, the team was fighting for a playoff spot so it was easy for you to look good." Except in this instance the Black Hawks weren't fighting for anything. And Harry knew it.

The next day he outlined a program for me that I was to follow the rest of spring and all summer. He'd carefully analyzed the Black Hawks and discovered what he felt to be their biggest weakness. "Maggy, there's no policeman on that team," he told me. "This is your opening. They need someone for the role."

So his main emphasis was on my learning to become a better fighter. I enrolled at once in a Denver karate school and began attending classes 7 to 9 P.M., three nights a week. A second grueling routine, which often lasted three hours, concentrated on overall conditioning. This I did in 13-day sequences. The fourteenth night Harry and I would go out together and have a ball. But then it was back for another 13-day cycle.

126

Harry and Me

There were all kinds of exercises in the program. Harry had written them down at the outset together with specific numbers for each. I went home and promptly doubled all the figures. As I've indicated before, I'm a sucker for punishment and wanted to prove that I was a lot tougher than Harry realized. The exercise I remember best is the same one Cliff and I still do when we go back to Denver each summer to condition ourselves for the season—running the steps in the football stadium. There are 105 of these, and I'd run them 12 to 15 times each night. I've pounded up those steps so many times I'm surprised the cement hasn't crumbled.

Sure it got monotonous, and was pretty lonely as well, running up and down those stairs in that big empty stadium. But I now felt driven. Any energy left whatsoever, and I'd pound those steps again. All the way up I'd be thinking, "One more time and I'll make the NHL." Or I might be hanging from the bar, struggling for that fifteenth chin-up. Pop! The NHL would come to mind. I'd pull myself right to the top. By pretending I was in the Chicago Stadium with the noise of the crowd echoing in my ears, I could psyche myself up beyond description.

In the summer Denver is pretty warm, and I'd just wear gym shorts for these workouts. Jogging along behind the stadium and past the hockey rink, I'd get that NHL feeling again and take off like a shot. Almost weightless, bouncing off the ground, happy. Nothing could stop me. I was all spirit.

The whole program had to take place at night, of course, because I had an eight-to-five job with a Denver realtor. Harry was a legal adviser in the firm. I was a bill collector. Age has its privileges after all. At the time Harry was a well-conditioned 33, and I barely 22. So evening was the only time I had for working out. People in the apartments across the way must have wondered what in hell was going on when they saw me prancing around, practicing my kicks and jabs in a mirror long after midnight.

Harry was always testing me on my progress. I'd arrive at work in the morning, and he or some other employee would pretend to throw a punch. My hands were now fast enough to block it, and I'd then proceed to go through a few of my moves: breaking up a little furniture, ripping a few suits. But Harry would smile. He knew I was gaining the kind of confidence an NHL policeman must have, and that I'd be ready by the time the Hawks' training camp opened in September.

One night my summer roommate, Bill Pettinger, and I were out on the town, when all of a sudden this carload of guys starts yelling at us. I've no idea what we've done. Well, before I knew it, I'm over there pulling open the driver's door. Boy, was I irritated! I just reached in, ripped the driver out from behind the wheel and hurled him over my leg in the process. Then I

went into my left-handed karate stance: right leg back
and rigid, left leg forward and slightly bent to permit
good balance for going either way. I was just about to
give him a big *"Keey—aaye!"* together with the heel of
my hand, when Bill Pettinger, who's a big fellow, pulled
me away. The others in that car never moved. And for
the first time, I believe, I truly appreciated that karate
is something you don't want to fool around with. But
the key point: I knew now that I'd be ready for the pros.

A few weeks before training camp, Harry bought
some rink time for a bit of practice. We chased up about
14 Denver area players, including Cliff and Jimmy
Wiste, who were back. Both had played the year before
with Chicago's Dallas farm club, the strongest in the
Central Hockey League. Cliff had accounted for 72
points in 78 games. Jimmy had scored 89! Not bad company for my trip to camp.

Harry still felt that one hole remained in my training:
growing accustomed to being hit behind my own net
and in the corners, something that hadn't happened
since my Canadian hockey days in Saskatoon. But what
I didn't know was that Cliff had been instructed to do
the familiarizing. Harry told him it would be a real ser-
vice if he'd run me every chance he had. Of course, this
helped Cliff too. And today he's known as one of the
hardest hitting wingers in the league.

He wasn't easy back then either. All I knew was that
suddenly Cliff seemed to be slamming me at every con-

ceivable opportunity. Could that first year in the pros have affected his mind, I worried? Anyway, I began running him back just as hard as I knew how. Once I even went out of my way to knock him down, and broke two ribs in the process.

At length we actually got into a heated incident, sort of a high-sticking affair, which was primarily my doing. We didn't drop gloves, but were shoving and elbowing each other like a couple of fledgling warriors. I'll admit I was pretty mad, until on the way back from practice, Harry told me about Cliff's orders: that he'd been doing me an enormous favor, whether I knew it or not. I felt like an idiot and told Cliff so. He simply nodded. "Wait till you get to Chicago," he said.

You can imagine how charged up I was the night before we left Denver. Cliff, Jimmy, Murray and me, our boss T. W. Anderson, Harry and wives all got together for dinner at Harry's house. All the conversation was about making the NHL, as if we could talk ourselves into it. After the party I lingered a moment with Harry and Vi, an older brother and sister to me. We all stood there with tears in our eyes. Then Harry just laid his hand on my arm. "Well, we've done all we can together. It's up to you now. You know what you have to do."

We checked in at Chicago's Bismarck, where the out-of-towners stay during training camp—ten days of morning and afternoon practices at the Stadium. Then a series of exhibition games until the regular season begins in late September. The hotel rooms are small and uncomfortable. That first morning I woke up at 4 A.M., sky high on nerves. By practice time I was so psyched up that each time Billy Reay blew his whistle I jumped about four feet.

Harry's two-part strategy began the moment I entered the Stadium. Normally, pro clubs take it easy the first three or four days to prevent such injuries as pulled groins. But the time for a novice to make an impression, said Harry, was during the first few days when the veterans are just getting back into it. Nothing would make Billy or Tommy Ivan happier than seeing a kid going full tilt even after "slow-down" orders had been issued. And it's true that in the middle of our first practice Billy did suggest to me that I take it easy. "You'll never last camp at the rate you're going," he said. But I thought of the steps back in Denver and knew otherwise. I just kept going full-speed ahead.

Harry's second and even more important point was for me to pick a fight early in camp to start building my "hit man" image as soon as possible. But under no circumstances should I come up against someone like Bobby Hull or Stan Mikita. This would make me look bad in everyone's eyes, like some punk trying to build his rep by slugging a star.

Toward the end of the first week, Harry phoned Cliff. "How's camp going?" Harry asked.

"Pretty good, I guess." An understatement in Cliff's case.

"How's Maggy doing?"

"Okay."

"Any fights yet?"

"Nope."

Less than a week later Harry phoned me: "Any fights yet, Maggy?" I reported a little shoving match with Eric Nesterenko in the corner during one practice. Nothing serious. We both skated away. And another time I'd pushed a hopeful like me, but that was the end of it.

In training camp you've really got to ream a guy to get him going. In other words, you've got to make it so obvious that you're after his job *and his pride* that you infuriate him to the point of retaliation. You simply have to hound him until you've forced him into it. Yet I didn't want to provoke this much hostility within the structure of a team I was part of. I just couldn't be that obnoxious, despite Harry's orders.

Four days later Harry came to Chicago himself. Management wanted to talk contract. He stayed at the Bismarck with us. It was the night before our first exhibition against Toronto at Maple Leaf Gardens. I'd had a good camp, but no fights. And I remember sitting in Harry's room, head down.

"What happened to our fight plan?"

I told him about my reluctance to tangle with my teammates. But then I found myself also confessing that these guys were a little bigger and tougher than I'd expected.

"Does that mean you're just a little afraid?" asked Harry very quietly.

"Yeah . . . a little," I admitted.

"Red," Harry said, "for the first time, I'm positive that now you really are prepared."

The next morning was gloomy, with low clouds disgorging one of Chicago's famous semidrizzles. Harry had an appointment with Tommy Ivan, to which I hadn't been invited. I was sitting on pins and needles. The team was departing for Toronto a little later for what would be my first real test. Maybe my last. I'd never felt so insecure in my life.

All the regulars were pretty well relaxed by now, looking forward to yet another season in their familiar team capacities. Quite a few of them were sitting around the breakfast area of the Bismarck that morning, clowning among themselves and eyeballing Harry and me huddled in the corner. We both felt pretty uncomfortable.

During any training camp there's only a small nucleus of players who are absolutely certain of their futures. Everyone else wonders where they'll be next week. Rumors are flying all the time. We all watch each other, and cast a particularly suspicious eye on any strangers. For two weeks, though, I kept telling myself I'd be staying right here.

Adding to our discomfort, Tommy's secretary informed Harry that Mr. Ivan had had to leave a little early for Toronto, but perhaps they might be able to get together later that night in Toronto. As it turned out, the first flight Harry was able to catch didn't get him to Maple Leaf Gardens until midway through the first period. And later he told me about overhearing such chance remarks as:

"Who the hell is that redhead anyway?"

"Yeah, who does he think he is!"

"Hmmm . . . Number 3 . . . Mag-new-san . . ."

"One of those chippy new kids."

It's true I was playing an all-out rough kind of game. Harry loved it. And he also noticed how the fans reacted to this Chicago player out there actually looking for trouble.

Then, late in the second period, I got into a substantial scrap with Toronto's Mike Walton. We exchanged a few good punches and both were chased for fighting. Harry called it a draw. But that didn't matter. Our fight plan was back on track and I'd just been welcomed to the NHL in the one way Harry had been sure would last.

To my immense delight I received the Star of the Game award that night. At Maple Leaf Gardens. I couldn't believe it. And leaving the dressing room, there's Harry and Tommy Ivan standing together down the corridor. I just waited near the door, feeling a bit awkward to say the least.

This had to be the showdown, however unlikely the setting. They must have been going over things like bonuses and number of years on the contract, because the basic salary figure wasn't going to be much of a problem, Harry had told me.

Tommy would listen, then walk off about 25 feet or so to ponder. Harry would smoke away with his foot up on one of those standing ashtrays. Obviously, both were planning their next moves. Then they'd be back talking again.

Days later Harry called me over and wrapped his arms around me. "Welcome to the NHL," he said. Tommy shook my hand and smiled. The tough negotiator's mask was back on the wall.

Cliff, Jimmy Wiste, Harry and I then went to a quiet tavern. No big celebration; just a few beers and a few moments of comfort. What really struck me, however, was that here were my friends as happy for me as if their own contracts had been settled.

Later that same night we were walking down Young Street looking for a place to eat. It was about 12:30 and we were trooping along single file because of this really narrow stretch of sidewalk beside a subway entrance. Harry was leading the group when suddenly up pops this diminutive figure in front of him.

"What the hell's going on here!" says this small silhouette.

"What's going on with you?" Harry replies, pleasantly but anxious.

"Who the hell are you?" barks this same figure just a little louder. By now Harry's patience is wearing thin, and we're all wondering how long this nonsense can go on.

"I'm Harry Ottenbriet," says Harry. "And you?"

"Billy Reay."

We were stunned. There goes my contract, I thought, and everybody's chances. Because Billy was more than a little upset.

"We're just looking around for a place to eat," Harry tries to explain, suddenly very apologetic.

"Like hell you are," says Billy. "You're Harry Ottenbriet and you're mishandling these hockey players of mine because you've kept them out till all hours of the morning." Of course, by this time we three had made an about-face and shortened the distance to our hotel by half.

Harry told me about the rest later. How he'd apologized for all of us, explaining that we'd been a little late because Keith had just signed. Suddenly Billy's whole manner changed, and his face broke into a smile.

"Boy, I'm glad that's out of the way," Billy said. And then the two of them fell into conversation like old cronies, talking about hockey and the league and Chicago's prospects for the coming season.

CHAPTER 6

The Riddler

It was at Denver that I began to write notes to myself, a trait I picked up from my dad, who's been a note writer all his life. With all sorts of new responsibilities and schedules to remember each day, I began carrying around sheaves of little paper slips addressed to myself. Hence my "Riddler" image, which persists to this day.

My college friends used to get a kick out of reading whatever memos happened to be lying around on my dresser or taped to the mirror. Typical would be one that began: "Wake up . . . wash face . . . brush teeth . . . eat breakfast . . ." I guess this must seem a little odd. But Cliff, who still spies on me, says that I've improved a lot since my college days; now I've at least eliminated the wake up instruction on my lists.

Without a list in my pocket I'm lost. It's as if I had two separate brains: the one in my head always skipping around open to everything like a butterfly, the other scribbled on paper in my pocket struggling to keep me organized with my feet on the ground. On the ice, however, they're at war with each other, and the consequences are often a riddle even to me.

For instance, I have a tendency to use words I don't understand but nevertheless like the sound of. So I've been guilty of some pretty severe malaprops. And what makes it worse, I also tend to talk in non sequiturs. Friends at college used to describe my conversation as "fade in, fade out."

I'll be carrying on with a train of thought and suddenly my mind goes racing off somewhere on its own. I then try to catch up with it, forgetting the conversation I left behind. So I do sometimes get stares from people as if I'm from outer space. I guess I do seem a bit drifty on occasion.

I've been told that I also suffer mental lapses. Cliff never lets me forget a particular trip to the track with Harry. Looking over the form listing the weights of jockeys and all, I somehow got the impression that the jockeys' weights were those of the horses. So I bet on this horse weighing 123 pounds. Well, I told Cliff and Harry about this a little later and they almost died. Of course, it struck me as pretty funny, too. P.S.: The nag won.

Absentmindedness is something else. I can be running an errand and completely forget what it's about

by the time I arrive. Take the situation with my tailor.
"My tailor." Sounds crazy. Why, no more than yester-
day, it seems, I only owned one suit. But today I have
twenty. Like most professional athletes, I'm very clothes
conscious. Our club is studded with sharp dressers—Pit
Martin and Stan Mikita most of all. Pride is frequently
reflected in one's appearance, and we're a pretty proud
bunch.

Anyway, I'll periodically rummage through my ward-
robe and try matching shirts and ties with different
suits. Not long ago when I was doing this, I noticed
the sleeves on several sport coats were too long. To be
trendy today, a man's shirt cuff ought to show about
half an inch, and with these coats on no shirt showed
at all. So I reached for my pad and scribbled, "Memo
to Keith . . . Right sleeve up ½ inch . . . left up ⅜ths."
My right arm has always been a bit shorter than my
left; probably because I'm left-handed. I then stuffed
the note in a lapel pocket.

That afternoon I stopped at Cosmo's, a tailor we like
to use, with this pile of jackets.

"Yes, Keith?"

"I'd like to have some work done," I began. "And,
uh . . ." Well, I'd completely forgotten what it was I
wanted done. Luckily, Cosmo knows my habit of writing things down. "That's all right," he says, starting to
hunt. Finally he discovers the memo in the lapel pocket.
"You don't have to say another word." Now when I go

139

in there, Cosmo just smiles and begins frisking my pockets.

My teammates love all this. I'm always getting kidded about skating barefoot or about my toebrush. Then there was the time I asked Louie, our equipment manager, for a pair of pliers to straighten my teeth. He thought I was kidding. You see, I'm forever after him, if not for a pair of pliers to straighten my teeth then to make sure he's carrying my weights along on road trips —or any one of a thousand other nit-picking concerns. Frequently he'll just look at me and sigh, "Okay, Maggy, what is it now?"

About those pliers, however. I was just being practical. Almost all hockey players have missing teeth and wear plates off the ice. Occasionally the teeth will loosen and start to flop around. Dentists can handle this, of course, but they cost money. Besides, just getting to a dentist in the middle of a season is a task all its own. So I've learned to turn the necessary wires on my plate to tighten my bite. What's so strange?

Once my tooth popped out at a banquet as I was attacking a roll. I scrambled around on the floor for a moment, found the thing and slipped it in my pocket. Okay. Until I had to address the group a short time later. I tried to offer an appropriate explanation, something about having tangled with a lot of noted pugilists but never having been really nailed until meeting one of their buns. Well, it was a try.

Anyway, back home I repaired the plate with a spot

of household cement, and it lasted two months. Of course there's a peculiar aftertaste for a few days. But it goes.

My unfortunate record with automobiles didn't end the night that house was demolished in Denver, I'm afraid. Regrettably, there've been several incidents since, a few of which I'm almost too embarrassed to mention. Cliff enjoys the time I decided to charge my battery by letting the car's engine run. Next morning we found the car completely out of gas and the battery stone dead. Cliff couldn't believe what I'd done.

Another time I drove a group of players somewhere. And when it came time to return home I took a taxi—forgetting my car. Oh well.

And there have been a few accidents, too. My mind simply tends to wander when I get behind the wheel. I don't know why. The summer after my rookie year, for example, I was waiting for Stan Mikita. We were going over to a Catholic church in the black district near the Stadium to play with a boys' softball league. The night before had been a late one and I got pretty drowsy waiting in my car, which was backed up close to a building. But I woke up when Stan passed by honking at me to follow him. I waved, put the car in reverse and backed right into the wall. *Crunch!* The bumper fell off. "Way to go, Alice," said Stan, appraising the damage. (He used to call me Alice because of my shot. Though now, I'm glad to say, he calls me Maggy.)

In the locker room where my mishaps were becoming

legend, I acquired the new sobriquet "Cale Yarborough," after the famous stock car champion. They'd add a number after the name each time. "Cale Yarborough #2 . . . #3 . . . #4 . . . etc."

A few nights after I'd become "Cale Yarborough #5" last year, I was bent over on the bench, working myself up just prior to game time. We were to play Philadelphia, I think. Not the biggest challenge in the league. Still, a good team will try to get up for every contest, and probably Tony Esposito and I work consciously at this more than anyone else. I call my own process "The Blue Funk." And at such times I always keep a pad of paper beside me to scribble down any extraneous items to be considered later. Because the one time I don't want *anything* to interfere with my concentration is during a hockey game. Jotting down these thoughts helps clear my mind.

Everyone knew about my latest accident, of course. It's become a ritual, in fact, for all the guys to visit the corpse of "Maggy's latest," and most of them had already made it over to the garage. On this occasion I'd been with Jerry Korab and we were sideswiped at high speed on the Kennedy Expressway. Pretty hair-raising, and the damage was quite spectacular. We'd been lucky.

So even though the players know enough not to bother me before a game, I could hear a lot of murmuring going on: "Geez, Cale's done it again!" . . . "Hey, don't you think he ought to enter the Demolition Derby?"

Lou-Lou Angotti looks across at Dennis Hull, who's lent me his car while mine is getting fixed. Normally Lou-Lou also withdraws before a game, and it's funny to watch him preparing to do so. He'll wipe his legs down with hot liniment and then put on his socks and wrap white tape around them. The final effect is that of a race horse leaving his stall for the track. "Washboard Louie," I call him. Not that he's overweight, but neither is he the skinniest player on the team.

So anyway, Washboard says, "Geezers, Dennis! How do you have the courage to lend Cale your wheels after that one?"

"I know," says Dennis, who can dead-pan with the best of them, "but I've got Lloyd's of London out on him."

It's about 10 minutes before game time. Now we're all just waiting quietly. Then Billy Reay comes in. He looks around the stalls for a minute making sure everyone's ready. Waits a minute for someone to finish doing up his skates. Pauses a moment or two more, until everyone is pretty well taken in by the game at hand. Then he claps his hands together: "Okay, let's go!" As we get up to move out, different players shout their pet phrases. Stan Mikita is usually first:

"Let's have a good warm-up!"

"Yeah, and keep the shots down," Dougie Jarrett will

add. "Stay out on the goalie! Let him get warmed up!"

"Get those legs moving, keep them moving!" Washboard Louie chimes in.

"And don't give them anything. None Against!" is invariably my addition.

When Dan Maloney first played with us, he'd just give out a loud roar, like the wild Irishman he is. And Bobby Hull, who was always the last one out the door, would slap each of us on the pants as we passed him. His was the last word: "And let's all go together, guys. It makes it easier."

Just before our locker room departure I had grabbed my pad and scribbled something. Someone whispered, "Hey, Tuna, get his notes. Let's see what he's writing."

"Tuna" Jarrett, Chairman of the Boards, sits right beside me. We call him Tuna because he gets a touch heavy in the off-season as he dreams about luxurious yachts and huge limousines, the kind top mobsters like Chicago's "Big Tuna" Accardo tool around in.

So Jarrett steals my pad. "Listen to this!" he says. "He's got 'Learn how to drive better!'" All the guys burst out laughing. The tension is gone. And we went on to cream the Flyers 6–2 that night.

Amazingly the very next day three of our guys had accidents. Trainer Skip Thayer, whom we called "Superman" because he resembles Clark Kent, banged a fender. "The Indian," Bryan Campbell, and Washboard Louie also managed a bit of damage on their own.

I'm a rather gullible fellow, as I guess I've confessed before. When defenseman Bill White first came to the Hawks from L.A., for instance, I asked him what he did in the off-season. In dead earnest, I thought, he said that he modeled Jantzen bathing suits. Bobby Hull and a few other players had been Jantzen models for quite a while, of course. But White's skinny legs are almost as ugly as mine. I mean, if he could model Jantzen, why couldn't I? Maybe there was hope after all. Several weeks later, however, I discovered the awful truth. He'd been putting me on. A cruel blow.

Bill's an amazing character. Though seemingly quiet and retiring, he has one of the sharpest wits around. And his defensive play, not so incidentally, is almost flawless. Vastly underrated, this oversight may well continue because of his unflamboyant style. Bill moves the puck with enviable grace.

Surprisingly, Bill White has only been in the league for 6 of his 14 professional years. In part this may be blamed on a five-year stint with Eddie Shore's Springfield Indians, once of the American Hockey League. Apparently this was professional hockey's Andersonville. Shore was an absolute tyrant, and playing for him was roughly equivalent to a career incarceration. To quote Alan Eagleson: "If the players were dogs, you'd pick up the phone and call the humane society."

Bill never mentions this himself. "Yeah, it was pretty rough," is about all he'll say. In addition to his modesty is his remarkable ability to psyche up for games just as if he were a rookie. Seeing such great desire in a 33-year-old pro is a true inspiration. And Bill's rock-solid temperament has a Gibraltarlike influence on the Black Hawks today. Recalling how Bill was labeled as one of Jack Kent Cooke's "bad apples" when he first joined us should indeed stir the ire of proponents for more truth in advertising. Just to show you how this kind of rot can set in, picture Bill and me bent way over in our stalls—concentrating like mad before the start of a big game. "Maggy," he murmurs, giving me a nudge of reassurance, "winning's the only way." This has now become one of my favorite expressions.

I've a set pattern of superstitions, which is by no means unique among athletes. Most players, in fact, have quite a variety of quirks. Like Billy Reay's different suits for different teams, for instance, or his thing about starting lineups. And, on the road, he'll hold team meetings in either his hotel room or the visitors' dressing room. If we've won the previous game in that city, we'll meet in the same place again. The spot changes if we lose.

Or consider Stan Mikita's habit of adding up the figures on car license plates in front of him to see if they equal 21, his jersey number. He also avoids certain lines on the ice during warm-ups and, like Pit Martin, insists that his training steaks be still faintly mooing.

Just about every player has a specific ritual he follows

before each game. And we're all so involved with our own quirks that we seldom really notice the next fellow's.

My own routine on a game day at home starts early in the morning. The list on my mirror begins with "game routine." I try to be as quiet as possible: I don't transact any business, and I don't make any phone calls. About 11 we meet at the Stadium. Then it's back to the apartment until late afternoon.

Cliff and I may watch the tube, or play a little Jackson Five or Roberta Flack. We eat our steaks promptly at 2, and if we talk at all, it's about the game. After eating, I usually lie down under my leopard and Cliff sprawls out under his zebra. We think about every man on the team we're about to play. And we may doze for a while. Then about 4:30 we'll have tea in silence and drive to the rink.

It's now that my heart really starts to pound, and my superstitions begin. On the way to the rink, I must not stop the car. Simply mustn't. If I see a red light ahead, I'll slow down so as to keep the car rolling. I've got to stay moving. And for three years I've always managed to do this. Going down the freeway, there's also that electric billboard flashing different items like the time and the temperature and "Listen to the Black Hawks . . . 8:15 . . . WMAQ." Before each game I have to see that last item. Simply have to. A few times I've had to slow down to a crawl in the emergency lane until this comes on. But we've not had any "Cale Yarboroughs" yet.

Rookie year, when Cliff and I would drive to most games together, there was a popular song that the disk jockeys were always playing. Every time we'd hear it, we'd win. It was amazing. And I remember driving to the Stadium one early spring afternoon. We were in the midst of that final run for the Prince of Wales Cup, where we won something like 15 straight games and "that song" had become our own private theme.

Here we were, everything going perfectly. No stops. The electric billboard sign right on schedule. But where's our song? It was our last game of the season. Against the Bruins. We had to have it. I was driving and Cliff started twiddling through all the stations searching desperately. Then, about four blocks from the Stadium, there it was. We broke into enormous smiles.

Suddenly Cliff says: "Hey, Maggy. Will ya close your window?"

"Sure, but why?"

"I'm afraid you're going to slap yourself to death with your lips."

Once I enter the rink, I begin my withdrawal. It's the only time that I'm a little cool with fans. Even the jokers on the team will usually then show consideration to the stone-face types like me. We've all been together long enough so that everyone is pretty much allowed to do his own thing. It's just a simple matter of mutual respect.

Doug Jarrett and I always dress in tandem. Given a winning streak, he'll pull on his left skate first and tighten the laces left over right. I'll do the same, only a few seconds later. If we lose, we switch to a right-before-left procedure. When I toss something at the trash bin about 15 feet away, it *must* go in. I'll keep trying until it does. Louie Varga *always* fixes my fighting suspenders for me. These have special snaps so that no one can yank your sweater over your head and punch you at will. Most players who get into scraps a lot wear them, and Louie's the one who does me up every time. Sometimes he'll then growl, "Okay, tough guy, remember to keep that thick head up and to land the first strike." Louie would make a fantastic boxer's second.

What I finally do just before hitting the ice is perhaps the most important part of my entire ritual. Though simple enough, it *has* to be done. We all file up that long, dark basement stairwell from the dressing room to the rink. Al Melgard on that giant organ right above us starts to play the team's music as 20,000 fans begin to roar their greeting. And I'm about to burst out on the ice surface, churning my legs just as hard as I can to get them moving. For me this is one of the biggest moments of every hockey encounter.

At the top of the stairs are two rail posts made of wood. Here I'll slip off a glove and rap on one twice.

Only once in three years have I missed doing this. And I was upset by it all night. I can't remember how we did, but before the next game I made sure to knock four times just to cover myself.

People are sometimes surprised how even-tempered and relaxed I am off the ice. I must seem schizophrenic, like Dr. Jekyll and Mr. Hyde. But Hyde only appears during games, and it takes a great deal of psyching to summon him up. And that's why I have to go through all the complicated pre-game business. Certainly this is one important difference between the game of hockey and the game of life. It takes years before one can measure one's accomplishments in the latter, but a hockey game lasts only 60 minutes—yet any number of goals can be achieved in this time. Sorry about the pun, but I think you'll find my meaning there. A fired-up Hyde then becomes Jekyll with the help of his bromides. These are waiting for me downstairs after the final buzzer.

Perhaps the biggest part of the riddle about me is wondering how a guy can be so stupid. Well, I don't feel entirely dumb deep down inside myself. And Dale once told me that it doesn't really matter how smart other people think you are just as long as you don't lack confidence in yourself. So who am I not to believe him? Apart from an occasional slip of the mind or two, I manage to stay in touch with what's going on in my own way. And if people want to laugh at my riddles, I'll go along with them.

I guess it all comes down to how you want people to regard you. And I've never minded my riddler's role, because if a bit of unity comes with the laughter, that's all to the good, isn't it? I never mind being a fall guy to achieve this.

CHAPTER 7

Inside a Team

I'm sad to hear about the surprising number of unpleasant incidents that happen between players on the
same team during the course of a season. A few are even
incredible. Just last year two Toronto defensemen, Jim
Dorey and Rick Ley, got into a brawl during an intra-
squad scrimmage. Maple Leaf coach John McLellan
nearly had his head removed trying to break them apart.
Poor Dorey—no favorite of mine, and a penalty baron
in his own right—had to be shot full of tetanus after
Ley almost chewed off his middle finger. He needed a
pair of Wayne's trapping mitts.

Of course, Toronto has been a losing team for quite a
few seasons now, so perhaps the strain is showing. I've
been fortunate never to play on a loser. But then, look
at a winner like New York. Right in the middle of last
season, here are Ranger veterans Pete Stemkowski and

Vic Hadfield tearing into each other, while speed-ball rookie Gene Carr and grisly Gary Doak go at it during the same practice. A month earlier, big Ken Hodge and little "Turk" Sanderson chopped each other in a lordly Bruins' workout.

These internal flare-ups make me just a little sick. Not that I'm unduly naive, because I know as well as anyone about the violent side of hockey. But fighting like this starts somewhere else. Maybe it's bad leadership or poor morale or conflicts that began back in the dressing room. I can truthfully say, however, that none of this has ever occurred on the Black Hawks in the three years I've been around.

Despite the fact that few things are sacred in the rough, mind-blasting atmosphere of a hockey game, one cardinal principle really must be observed at all times: a player's loyalty toward his teammates. You should always be playing for interests larger than your own. And if you get traded to another team tomorrow? Well then, that becomes your team and you give it the same 100 percent. Of course I've never been traded either, so maybe I'd better just talk about what goes on inside the Black Hawks.

To begin with, we're a funny team both on and off the ice. We work hard; yet we have a great deal of fun. And this is what teamwork is all about—laying things on the line together with jokes and laughter. In this way few tensions develop, and there's no real friction to speak of.

None Against!

During a recent red vs. white road scrimmage, for example, we discovered that we didn't have a complete set of jerseys along. Consequently a few of us had to wear sweaters that weren't our own. Cliff is in my red #3. I'm wearing his white #20. Jarrett has on Dennis Hull's white #10. Dennis has Dougie's red #4. It's a natural setup for a bit of clowning, and so after the scrimmage begins we each decide to imitate a few of the other's notable characteristics.

Dougie and Dennis, whom we call "Frere" because he's so tired of being "Bobby Hull's younger brother," are the team's outstanding comedy duo. Dougie, however, refers to Dennis as "Blue-line Hull" for his habit of tripping over the enemy blue-line.

So here comes Jarrett in Frere's #10 rushing headlong down the ice. But the moment he hits the attacking blue-line he does this spectacular flip. And Dougie, who once took figure-skating lessons, can really toss his body around.

Dougie, on the other hand, is noted for his low pain threshold. A splinter requires major surgery and great anguish. Or he'll get hit in the foot and just go out of his mind, hopping and limping about like a madman. So here's Dennis suddenly pretending he's blocked a shot with his ankle. He drops to the ice moaning, clutching his skate, and begins a spastic crawl toward the bench.

Naturally I am pretending to be Cliff. No way to

make my ears any larger, so I'm exaggerating his habit of rebounding off the corner boards like a crazy man in a padded cell, taking down everyone around me. Cliff, in turn, has adapted my quirk of jerking my knees just before face-offs. It's the special way I set to go in any direction. So every time Billy prepared to drop the puck, here's Cliff in this ridiculous bow-legged stance shaking his legs up and down as if he had Saint Vitus's dance. Perhaps the best performance of all.

There's a lot of this sort of thing. Like the practice right after "Heiskala Night," when I'd scored my first regular season goal and put Heiskala out of commission. Remember? I'd been so happy about the goal that I'd thrown my gloves way up in the air. Well, the next day everyone is skating around shaking out their legs when suddenly the whole team throws their gloves in the air. Lou-Lou Angotti skates by me muttering, "What kind of crap is that, you showboat!" Though everyone is laughing, of course. (Bobby Hull would even have my scoring puck gold-plated and present it to me with Earl Heiskala's tooth mounted right in the center.)

Angotti loves to get your goat during practices. Last season, for example, he was always getting around "King Kong" Korab in one-on-one drills. Jerry would stand there in complete frustration afterwards pounding his stick on the ice. "Come on down again, you little Wop!" he'd yell. Sure enough, here'd come Lou-Lou streaking down on him again—perpetual motion as usual: more movements than a grandfather clock.

"You'll never touch me, you big gorilla," he'd say just before faking around Korab once again.

Our most accomplished dressing room entertainers are Dennis and Dougie. They're always working together on new routines. Much of their material comes from such TV shows as "Laugh-In" and "All in the Family," or commercials like "I can't believe I ate the whole thing." And they are always doing takeoffs on prominent political figures. It's truly professional stuff, which they'll pull off right in the middle of normal conversations or in the bus going to and from the airport.

One of their best ever was a skit called "Buzz." This was after a trip to New York when we'd arrived there early enough the night before to drop in on a Buster Mathis training session. Everyone was impressed. Mathis, of course, is a huge man, and when he'd lay into that bag, the whole room would shudder. So our next stand was in Toronto, and here's Dennis in the locker room, wearing a pair of black silk shorts, popping the air in an extravagant bob and weave. Meanwhile, Jarrett is carrying on like a ringside announcer.

"Way to go Buzz! You're looking sharp! That's a right to the head! Left to the body! Right uppercut! Oh Buzz, what a combination!" This patter continues for some time, and there wasn't a dry eye in the house.

Dennis has had to suffer a lot of static, living in the

shadow of his fabulous brother. The fans would boo him for the slightest wrong. However, Billy stuck by him through thick and thin, waiting for him to gain confidence and break out on his own—which he did, as Dennis has now become a star.

Dougie is my defense partner, so I'm especially close to him. During the first half of my rookie year I roomed and played the ice with Whitey Stapleton. Then Billy switched me to Dougie, and we've been together ever since. From the beginning he took me under his wing. Sometimes he'd be furious when I was goaded into a pointless fight. "Let's stay on the ice, damn it!" he'd growl. "It's hard on the rest of us. Plus it screws me up having to go on with someone else." Except then he'd add with that little smirk of his, "But don't stop fighting altogether. Just pick your spots more carefully."

We'd talk a lot on the bench. And if the game was going badly, we'd try to figure out the reasons. If the game was going well, we'd just cheer each other on.

"You think too much, Maggy," Dougie would tell me. "Don't overpsyche yourself now." And I soon learned that if we were in the middle of a winning streak, Dougie doesn't like to talk about it. He's got his superstitions too.

We drink a fair number of ice cream floats on the road. I'll fetch Dougie any flavor he wants as long as he puts it in Seven-Up. Perhaps this started as a favor to me, but now he likes it. And if one of us makes a mistake in the game, the other guy usually blames himself. "I've paired with a lot of guys," he once told me, "but when I see how serious you get, I want to play even harder." This is one of the finest compliments I've ever received, and it's the kind of feeling that makes a team great. Dougie has been like an older brother to me. And I sincerely regret being picked for the All-Star squad the last two years when Dougie hasn't been. "Nonsense!" he'd say.

I'm always asking him about marriage and life and things. And he'll tease me on the manners and figures of the girls I date. There's an expression he has for those who are exceptionally well endowed. "Maggy," he'll say with that choir-boy expression of his, "now there's a real pair of lobsters."

Then he'll ask when I'm going to get married. And I tell him I don't know, that I don't feel ready to be around the same person all that much. Nor have I found the right girl. It's just not my time yet.

"Don't worry," he assures me. "You'll find her. You'll know when the time comes."

Doug Jarrett had to grow up pretty fast. He got married at 18 and now has five kids. He tells me how important his family is to him: how much his wife, Marilou, has helped him.

Often on the road he'll ring her up after a game, particularly a winner. We'll be sitting in the room with our ice cream floats and he'll ask her, "Did you see the game,

Marilou? . . . Maggy and I thought we played pretty well." Then Marilou will needle him playfully, something like, "Yeah, but what happened against Jones?" if Jones happened to have scored against us.

"Well, I guess I was napping on that one," Dougie will admit. Or she'll ask, "What happened to Maggy in his fight? Is he okay?" Dougie will just look over at me and laugh. "Honey, you couldn't hurt that head with a sledgehammer."

In the practical joke department, no one can top Whitey Stapleton or Stan Mikita: whether it's swapping false teeth in the locker room or stealing shoes on a plane trip. And everybody is fair game except Billy Reay.

On the road, Whitey once lifted a reporter's typewriter. A few days later he hid an all-important microphone of the WGN Channel 9 crew that broadcasts all our road games. Still another time, when CBS was doing a Black Hawks' special in Montreal and producer Bruce Roberts received a bogus telegram saying that production costs were much too high and that he should bring his crew back immediately, Whitey's involvement was strongly suspected.

But late last season Whitey finally got his comeuppance when, on the way back from a long road trip, *his* shoes disappeared for a change. Whitey refused to leave the plane without them, and padded up and down the aisle for almost an hour until a skycap discovered them

159

on an empty ticket counter and delivered them to the almost deserted aircraft far out on the runway. Everyone else was now home in bed.

But Whitey says he's got the names of all those responsible, and promises a very special revenge for them. Maybe some night after Toronto or Montreal each of these guys will be stopped at customs and something terrible found in their luggage. Whitey will go to any lengths for a joke, despite which he's still an immensely popular team leader.

The time I laughed the hardest at one of his stunts was during training camp. This can be a fairly scary period, and anything that breaks the tension a little is welcome. So during lunch period Jimmy Pappin settles into the Stadium's organ loft. We all call him "Bird" because of his beak; and he's an athletic nut. His closest friends are all baseball players, golfers or football types. He could be good at almost any sport and is a man of many talents.

Anyway, all the veterans knew that "Bird" was taking a do-it-yourself course at home and learning to play the organ by the numbers. Shades of Denny McLain. So here he sits down at what purports to be "the world's largest music maker" and begins to play. Fantastic music! Everyone is shocked. He'd only begun two months ago. His fingers are twiddling and he's leaning way over and his feet are pumping the pedals. Great

Scot! I was thinking. Jimmy's some kind of a genius!
Maybe he's missed his true calling.

Well, the whole thing is an elegant put-on masterminded by Whitey Stapleton. Whitey had located a
tape done by the regular Stadium organist, Al Melgard,
and persuaded Bird to go through the motions while it
was playing on the speakers.

Whitey is also a very practical person. Last year in
the playoffs when the league suddenly became so particular about the width, curve and length of sticks that
an official had to put his personal inspection stamp on
each stick before every game, Whitey discovered his
stick blades weren't quite wide enough. So the day of
our first game against Pittsburgh, here's Whitey attach-
ing strips of balsa wood to his blades with airplane
cement. And the sticks passed inspection with no questions asked.

Whitey is the team's fastest dresser. Sometimes he
doesn't get to the Stadium until 10 minutes before practice. Whenever a player is late for a session, everyone
bangs his stick on the ice to draw Billy's attention to
him. But Whitey always steps on the ice with just a few
seconds left. And we all give him a big hand. Incidentally, another player who's a master at timing is our other
outstanding goalie, Garry Smith. Between each period
of every game, he strips off all 40 pounds of his equipment and sits around in his birthday suit, then manages

161

to get everything on before we take the ice again. Amazing.

"Stosh" Mikita's brand of humor is more a virtuoso effort. For sheer unpredictable wit, he's hard to touch. A good example came at the end of my rookie year when we were down to the last weekend of the Prince of Wales race against Boston. It was the hottest battle in league history.

Sports Illustrated was covering the story, and their cover was to be either "Little Joe" Sanderson or me, depending on which team won. Well, we ended with an identical 99 points for the season. But since the Hawks had won 45 games to the Bruins' 42, my picture appeared on the SI cover, missing tooth and all. Stan got a blowup of this and gave it to me with *Mad* magazine's caption, "What? Me Worry?" dubbed in. Funny man.

When Stan is in the mood he's like a happy little boy, waltzing around the rink during lulls in the practice, playfully tripping guys, rubbing his glove in your face or pretending to pick a fight. One morning I wrestled him to the ice. "Don't bite off more than you can chew, kid," he said. Lesson learned.

Stan is a polished actor. About an hour before a game, for example, he'll pull this funny little Hitler bit—wearing a long trenchcoat, small piece of black tape across his upper lip, his hair combed down. The Nazi salute. Then: "You *vill* play dis game und you *vill like it!* . . .

You *vill vin* und you *vill like that too!*" He has any number of stunts up his sleeve, and his timing is superb.

Because Stan is a pretty sarcastic fellow and has this fake little laugh that can be interpreted in any number of ways, it's hard to tell when he's serious. This keeps us all on our toes. Still, no one is a more successful teacher with hard-working, receptive rookies.

Mikita is also one of the finest playmakers in the game. He sets up goals that the scorer never sees coming. Suddenly, there's the puck just lying on his stick almost like a three-cushioned billard. Part of Stan's secret is mixing his moves, and this he does like a skilled baseball pitcher. He's all wire and ball bearings out there. Being small, he takes a terrific amount of punishment. But he doesn't let it pass unrewarded. Like Gordie Howe, Stan keeps his own records and has a million subtle ways to square accounts.

His humor is seldom without a point. I mean, consider when Pit Martin returned to the team after all those accusations he'd made about the special privileges being accorded super-stars like Stan. The locker room could have been a pretty tense place, right? Slow burns and resentment building up. But this evaporated the first day of training camp when Mikita went right over to Martin. "Hello there," he said. "You must be Hubert Jacques Martin, the fellow they call 'Perfect Pit.'" No one, of course, had ever called him that before. But it

163

was typical Mikita: a neat, fast way of breaking the ice. And it describes Pit pretty accurately too.

Pit really does believe that what he says is right. And he was certainly right in pointing out that everyone on the same team should be treated the same. It's just common sense—which, incidentally, Pit exhibits a lot of on the ice. He can also take off from a dead stop faster than any player I know.

But getting back to Stosh again. When Bobby Hull finally ended his holdout, he'd missed all of training camp and the regular season had actually begun. Once more this might have produced strains throughout the team. But again, Mikita forestalled any possible estrangement. And perhaps I should add here that despite all the rumors about frictions and jealousies between Mikita and Hull, they simply didn't exist.

Earlier that summer, Bobby had been in Europe visiting several foreign countries including Yugoslavia. The day he arrived in Belgrade, that city's newspaper had a picture of him on the front page with a headline reading: BOBBY HULL FAMOUS FOOTBALL STAR ARRIVES!

Well, Stan had procured a giant blowup of the picture with the headline translated. And there it was waiting in Bobby's locker stall when he entered the dressing room. Hanging on a hook right next to it was an ancient leather football helmet and an old pair of figure skates with tiny cleats instead of blades.

What an impact that made on me as a rookie. It said

more about team spirit than words could. When flashy Chris Bordeleau came to us from St. Louis, he put his finger on it. "A sophisticated team" was the phrase he used. I like that. We represent an enormous latitude of individuality, but we can put it all together on the ice. And isn't this what "sophistication" really means—collective know-how.

Now that Bobby Hull has gone to Winnipeg in the recently organized World Hockey Association, everyone asks me about him. Well, how can I say we're not going to miss the strongest man in hockey with the finest wrist and slapshot combination the game has ever seen? We're going to miss him terribly. Bobby is the ideal team man. Also he's been the best "hockey salesman" in NHL history, which certainly didn't hurt our box office. And all these years he's given it everything he had. The Golden Jet is indeed the Babe Ruth of hockey.

Bobby deserves to have made a fortune from this sport, which has been his whole life. I know that I speak for all his former teammates. As Cliff has said: There's no way you can fault him for making a choice that will guarantee he need never work another day in his life if he doesn't want to. For a true professional, the decision is as clear as black and white. We'd all have done the same in his lucky shoes. More power to him.

True, he's left a tremendous void. But we're a great team, and even a loss such as his won't crush our spirit. After all, he'll be back: dropping in on us from time to time, probably with one of those cattle pamphlets he was always reading tucked in his pocket, looking over our plates to see if someone's left any meat; and if he finds any potatoes, eating those as well. My God, what an appetite! We called him the human "garborator"— an imaginary disposal machine. But what I'll remember most about Bobby is his endless generosity to everyone, plus all those professional farm-boy sayings.

Two things that happened early my rookie year told me a lot about Bobby. Our trainer Skip Thayer (where's Skip? he's over Thayer), a punster, was just settling into the Chicago area for the first time. He'd located an apartment for his wife Nancy and their two children, but was low on funds for the initial deposit. The team was about to go on an extended road trip and it would be several weeks before Skip got his next pay check. The situation was a tight one.

Skip, quite naturally, keeps his personal matters pretty much to himself. But on a team as close as ours, an individual's problems travel by osmosis. Information seems to come right out of the walls. So after our last home practice, Bobby, who's been lingering and fiddling around with his equipment, just happens to be the last player to leave. Finally, when only he and Skip are together, Bobby slips an envelope into his hand containing the exact amount of cash Skip needs for his deposit, an unsolicited loan from Bobby's own pocket.

"Hope this helps a little, Superman," Bobby said with

that irresistible wink and magnetic grin. Skip will never forget the moment.

Bobby, in fact, is always up to this sort of thing. I remember the first time I tailed him through a crowd while he was being mobbed, as always, by fans who just wanted his big "B. H." autograph and a smile. Bobby never failed to oblige. But afterwards, he'd hand over the autograph pad or program to any teammate down to the lowliest rook. This first time, when he did it to me, I could hardly believe it. Today, I realize that he's simply a great star who has kept his feet on the ground.

Chico Maki, who was Bobby's silent partner for a decade, will miss him the most, of course. They hung around together all the time, Chico strumming his guitar and humming the Johnny Cash songs he likes. Chico, Bobby's great playmaker, sitting there in his boots, smoking his pipe and talking about the old T-Bird he completely restored himself. Chico's a fireman in the off-season and just loves to work on engines. He's always got a car project going. It was fun to hear Bobby and Chico together, Chico telling him all about his T-Bird, Bobby telling Chico all about his latest breeding bulls.

And what moments of glory they shared together on the ice! One time I shall always remember was the 1970–71 All-Star game when the West Division team was predominantly a Black Hawks' contingent. The East was loaded and super-cocky. As the Rangers' Brad Park said before the game, "How in hell do those Western guys think they've got a chance in this one?" Except Bobby and Chico must not have heard him, because in the first five minutes of the contest each had a goal. Final score: West 2, East 1.

After the game we all were sitting in the Boston Garden's "West" dressing room. Bobby looks over at Tony O, Bill White, Pat Stapleton, and me. "Way to go, Defense!" he says. And we came back with the customary reply we use after every Black Hawk winning game: "Way to go, Offense!"

That night we showed the league a little of the Black Hawks' spirit.

But I'm sure Chico will adjust to Bobby's jump in the same quiet, businesslike way he's been playing all these years. Bobby may have gone to Winnipeg all right, but one of the almost silent blessings is that Chico Maki—guitar, T-Bird and all—is still with Chicago.

I might add here that all of us believe the WHA is a help to hockey. Perhaps it will take 10 years before the new league is really solid. But Bobby's money shows they're not kidding; and in the long run, it may do for hockey what Sonny Werblin's huge deal to Joe Namath did for the AFL and, ultimately, for pro football. Even now, it gives every decent player in the NHL a little extra bargaining power for salaries commensurate with the entertainment we provide and the considerable risks we take.

Almost every NHL player has been "drafted" by a

WHA team just as Bobby was picked by Winnipeg. So you'll frequently hear us joking about the WHA in the locker room. Maybe a player has just been chewed out in private by Billy Reay for some dumb move. "Well, see you in the WHA," we'll tell him. Or perhaps some disagreement arises with management and you'll hear a player say, "I'll bet the Winnipeg Jets don't do it like that!"

I'd hate to leave Chicago. For one thing, I can't imagine finding a better team. For another, I don't believe even the most hard-nosed professional hasn't some sentiment for the team that's done all the things Chicago has done for me. Besides, I'd have to find something new to knock on just before games. Seriously, though, you do become pretty attached to a spot—especially if you're a creature of habit like me.

For starters, there's the Stadium itself. The first time I saw it I was reminded of one of those castles I used to dream about, just standing there with those sculptured lions in the corners and surrounded by open space. It's not a pretty place, but it's distinctive nevertheless. And when they put up those banners—"Home of the Black Hawks" . . . "Eastern Division Champions" . . . "Winners of the Western Division"—the Stadium even becomes beautiful. The only pennant that hasn't flown in my time is "Stanley Cup Champions." We came so close that I could actually see it up there. But we'll get it yet. You can bet on that.

None Against!

One's own rink is like a second home after a while. You get to know all its moods, its lights and shadows. There's the game mood that's a lot like a giant party with 20,000 celebrants roaring and having a time for themselves. But practice the next day is like the morning after. No one's there at all. The rink is a cold and solitary place then, echoing any number of moods I may be feeling.

I can understand why so many athletes go into a decline after their days have passed. Like an actor who has lost his stage. No more attention, no more parties, no more being made to feel like a god all the time. Suddenly it's over and your voice sounds hollow and small like in an empty stadium. The athlete must plan his life so that he never feels dropped off the edge like this, so that there will always be new goals to conquer and other horizons to cross after the cheering stops.

There will always be other things for me. And I believe what I enjoy most is working with people. Bobby Hull taught me this—the very real satisfaction a person gets when he gives of himself to others. One such example are the neighborhood kids who hang around the Stadium exits hoping to see us. The whole area is a depressed black community with more serious concerns than following our hockey schedule. Nevertheless, the kids show a lot of feeling for the players. I give them old practice sticks once in a while as well as some of my Seven-Up promotional pucks, and it's enormously touching to see them trying to adapt to a foreign game in the vacant lots around the area. Here they are on roller skates wearing torn old jerseys, magazines strapped to their shins for guards, and using old sticks with a tennis ball or pop can for a puck. I stop and watch them from time to time; a few are really great little stick-handlers.

There's one kid named Chico who's about twelve years old. He is always around. After every game he seems to know exactly how things have gone, though I don't think he's ever been inside the Stadium. He'll tell me just how I've played, and calls me "Champ" like all the other kids.

After we'd won one night, I gave him five dollars. I was so happy that I simply wanted to make his day a little brighter. He disappeared in tears. But he still speaks of that night. Today we're good friends, and whenever I've played badly he really lets me have it.

"Man, you just don't know how to fight, do you?" Or, "What's the matter, Champ? You going chicken or something?" Then he'll smile and pat me on the back.

Blacks have yet to make it into the NHL, but it will happen. It has to. Just look at the way they've taken to every other sport once they've had exposure to the facilities and received some coaching. In hockey, of course, these are still both expensive and hard to find. But make no mistake. Where there's an interest, there will be good hockey players someday. For instance, at rehabilitation centers and veterans hospitals, where I talk a lot with black patients, I'll ask, "Do you watch hockey?"

"We sure do!" they'll answer with broad grins.

"Well, it's nice meeting you," I'll say. "I'm Keith Magnuson of the Chicago Black Hawks."

"Man, you don't have to tell us that! You're the fighter." They know what's going on.

The truth is, I've begun to feel that a person's attitudes about teamwork are conditioned by the community in which he lives. Not that a big-city environment will ever be like a small-town situation. But there are many small towns, communities, in Chicago. And lately I've been trying to get around to as many of them as possible.

Of course, some of this is simply part of my job. But I still love to be with groups of kids. I'll tell them a bit about my background, maybe a few Wadena stories to illustrate what the NHL really means to a young Canadian. Then a little about Denver, stressing the value of a college education. Sometimes I'll hear a few of the younger ones getting restless, whispering in the front row such things as, "I'm going to get him to sign my hand." So I'll throw in a few "riddler" stories. These recapture their attention and also help get one of my favorite points across: It's important to learn to laugh at yourself early in life.

Invariably, everyone wants to hear about my fighting

and, of course, who I hate the most. I try to point out my entirely separate roles on and off the ice. I stress that it's seldom a matter of hating as much as it's the specialized kind of job I do for the team. I'm not sure the younger ones can grasp this distinction. Still I don't want them to think that following my fighting example is necessarily a positive thing to do. Perhaps that's sort of hypocritical, but at least I try.

Somebody too will always ask me about my teeth. And I'll tell them about the hard roll incident and my do-it-yourself dentistry techniques and how I actually lost the tooth when a teammate cross-checked me during a practice at Denver, then almost cried about it afterwards because he felt so sorry. At one appearance, for instance, this tiny little kid asked: "Mr. Magnuson, I saw a picture of you once with a missing tooth. How come they're all there now?" I simply clicked out my plate with the top of my tongue for him.

"Gee," he murmured, "that's really cool!"

I'll usually wind up with a hockey story. A particular favorite of mine concerns a playoff between Heaven and Hell. The Devil and Archangel Gabriel are together in the press box before the game watching the teams warm up. The Hell squad all have "D's" on their jerseys for "Devils." Heaven's team have "A's" for Angels."

"Let's see," says Gabriel. "You've got Derek Sanderson (*"Boooo!"*) . . . the Hextall brothers (*"Boooo"*) . . .

None Against!

Eddie Shack (*"Boooo!"*) . . . Barclay Plager and "Busher" Watson (*"Boooo!"*)

And the Devil says, "Yes, but you've got some pretty tough players too. There's Bobby Orr . . . Jean Ratelle . . . Stan Mikita . . . Tony O . . . Dougie Jarrett . . ."

"But," interrupts the Devil, rubbing his horns and looking puzzled, "Who's your player, Gabe, with the BH on his jersey?"

"Oh, him!" says Gabriel. "That's God, and he thinks he's Bobby Hull."

All ages understand this one. And the fact that Bobby's no longer with Chicago doesn't mean I'm going to change the story. His name means "team" in anyone's language. It really doesn't matter who he's playing for.

Perhaps the final measure of a great team, though, is how deeply the players feel about one another. Naturally, this brings me back once again to my old buddy, Cliff, who's recently gone off and married a lovely creature named Lynnae. There's no tragedy in this for either of us. In fact, I couldn't be happier. At least I won't have to suffer through so many "Lips" jokes anymore. Seriously, however, I suppose the only real sadness between us would be if we found ourselves playing on different teams.

When I first began this book, it was a totally different kind of challenge to me, and naturally I'd go over a lot of the material with Cliff as we went along. Once I asked him about titles. "I think you should call it

"Keith's Roommate, Cliff," he replied, trying not to laugh. But in a very real way he's right. Our friends haven't been calling us "The Odd Couple" for nothing. Even Billy Reay refers to us as "The Gold Dust Twins." Cliff always did our cooking and I'd do the cleaning. I'm going to have to take a Julia Child cram course in cooking now that I'm living alone.

But we complimented each other well. Cliff was always the silent and serious side of the arrangement. While I tend to be more flamboyant, and will ramble on like an old woman if given half a chance. So then I get more than my share of the limelight and attention. Cliff has certainly shown an extraordinary amount of character.

We'd never yell at each other. Not that we never had differences. It's just that we're so competitive most of the time that if there's anything bothering us we try to settle it on the ice. So sometimes during practice we'd really belt each other, usually over some stupid little thing that had started back at the apartment. Otherwise, we'd settle our arguments via the silent treatment. Except by the next morning, we'd be friends again.

I guess the time I got maddest at him was once in Montreal. We were both out for that optional morning skate the day of the game. Cliff was just fooling around, and he flipped a puck at me. It hit the top of my head for six stitches. I was madder than hell as I stomped off the ice bleeding like a slaughtered pig.

175

None Against!

Skip Thayer wrapped my head in a big turbanlike compression bandage. At first I looked like an Arabian sheik, then later, with my long maxi-overcoat on, like a wounded Gestapo officer. When Stan first saw me he snapped to attention and raised a stiff right arm: "Sieg Heil!" Everybody laughed. I was furious.

Cliff kept telling me all afternoon how sorry he was, but I wouldn't talk to him or anyone else. Then, about an hour before game time, when I realized I was behaving like an ass, it was my turn to do the apologizing. "Sieg Heil!" saluted Stan, clicking his heels.

Only one time did Cliff's and my keen sense of competition really get me into trouble. This was when I was taking those boxing lessons at Johnny Coulon's Southside Chicago gym, and thought I'd pass on a few pointers to Cliff. Well, the press got hold of the item, and the boom descended the morning we were to leave on a road trip. I was called into Billy's office, where I found him staring at a sports page headline: MAGNUSON TEACHES BOXING TO KOROLL IN APARTMENT. Headlines, mind you!

"Good God, Maggy," Billy fumed, "What *the hell* are you trying to do? What do you expect to teach youngsters in the U.S.?"

I came out almost crying because I'm very sensitive to anything Billy says. "Hey there, Mag," Bobby Hull told me. "Don't take it so hard." He was using that reassuring, "Way to go, Man-o'-War" tone of voice, and it settled me down pretty well.

But then when we got to Boston, there it was again: headlines . . . MAGNUSON TAKES BOXING LESSONS— WON'T BACK AWAY FROM ANYONE; NOT EVEN OWN ROOMMATE! The same story in Philadelphia. Same thing in Toronto. I was ready to die. Billy never said another word, but I knew what he was thinking. Finally I went into him and blurted, "You *know* I didn't have anything to do with this, don't you?" First he stared at me a little while. Then he nodded. Finally he smiled.

But the time with Cliff I'll remember as long as I live was late summer after my knee operation, when my whole leg was still in its ankle-to-hip cast. In terms of true friendship, this became the most significant moment of my life.

Early in May, we'd lost the seventh game of the Stanley Cup finals to Montreal by a single goal after leading the series 2–0 at the start. No other team in history had ever made it back from such a deficit. Trying to be somewhat philosophical today, perhaps it's appropriate that the team from the spot where hockey all began should have been the first to make such a comeback. Never mind. All I knew at the time was that Henri Richard got around me to score the winning goal in a series that we had led two to zip.

Later people made excuses for me. My knee problem, for one. The stiffness and the pain. Richard had picked up the pass coming straight off his bench. Never mind that either. As I've said, I don't buy alibis. All that counted was that I was too slow trying to cut him off. He passed me and scored. At least I should have tripped him which in the third period of a tied-up Stanley Cup final would have been a *good* penalty.

After the game I felt the most terrible and isolated moment I've ever known. The entire team was in tears. But right then, inside myself, the sense of personal guilt was complete. I wanted to quit everything. I was washed up in hockey. I wasn't fit to work as a Seven-Up executive. I had no business standing in front of kids. I was going to move away from Chicago . . . somewhere very far away.

Things would change, of course, but the weeks that followed were to be the rockiest of my life. And frankly, I don't know what I'd have done without Cliff. After my operation, he ferried me around, always available, always ready to help. Then one summer evening when I was still on crutches, we went to a Chicago nightspot where we both like to relax. And, sure enough, here's some loud-talking clown who can't wait to start raking over the entire Montreal series. He keeps getting closer and closer to his point until finally he just lets me have it: "And what *the hell* happened to you *anyway*, Magnuson?"

I had no special urge to hit him, in spite of the way he was baiting me. Because one of the things you quickly learn as a professional athlete is not to go around popping people; you either sit there and take it from some creep or quietly leave.

Suddenly I found myself outside standing on crutches in the rain crying. All the sorrow and humiliation of that Richard goal was back to haunt me again in full force. The guilt whirling around in my head once more. I could have done anything to myself that night.

Cliff appeared from nowhere. He hadn't seen me leave the place, but someone told him I'd wandered off and he immediately rushed outside. To hell with the car, he said. He grabbed a cab and piled me in. When we got home he carried me up the stairs and helped me into bed.

I lay there, pools of light swimming on the ceiling, coming from the street lamps through the rain-spattered windows. Then suddenly I heard "our song," the same one Cliff and I used to hunt for on the radio driving to the Stadium. Cliff must have slipped it on the stereo.

I began to relax, everything unwinding in my body. It was as if I were lying on air, like those times I'd be running back in the dark from the steps in Denver and would get a spurt of energy thinking about the NHL.

I began to think about hockey again. About the next season coming up and all the seasons to follow. Right then I suddenly realized that part of being a true professional is learning to leave all your karma and guilt behind and not to carry your losses around like an enormous bag of yesterdays: the one thing that Bobby Hull *never* did.

I became so excited, in fact, that I almost picked up the phone and called Harry. "Harry," I would have told him, "now I'm *really* ready! I've finally learned."

"Learned what, Red?"

"Learned what every pro's got to know. What every member of a team has to do. . . ."

"Okay, okay. *What?*"

"I've *finally* learned how to live with a defeat."

I never did call Harry, of course. Instead, I hobbled to the door leading into the living room. Cliff was sitting on the couch.

"Thanks, pal," I said to him.

"Anytime," he answered. "But stop smiling. Your lips are hiding your face."